THE FOOD AND COOKING OF ROME AND NAPLES

THE FOOD AND COOKING OF ROME AND NAPLES

65 CLASSIC DISHES FROM CENTRAL ITALY AND SARDINIA

VALENTINA HARRIS

PHOTOGRAPHY BY MARTIN BRIGDALE

aquamarine

This edition is published by Aquamarine
an imprint of Anness Publishing Ltd,
Blaby Road, Wigston,
Leicestershire LE18 4SE

Email: info@anness.com

Web: www.aquamarinebooks.com;
www.annesspublishing.com

If you like the images in this book and would like to investigate using them for publishing, promotions or advertising, please visit our website www.practicalpictures.com for more information.

PUBLISHER'S NOTE
Although the advice and information in this book are believed to be accurate and true at the time of going to press, neither the authors nor the publisher can accept any legal responsibility or liability for any errors or omissions that may have been made nor for any inaccuracies nor for any loss, harm or injury that comes about from following instructions or advice in this book.

Publisher: Joanna Lorenz
Editor: Kate Eddison
Copy Editors: Catherine Best and Jan Cutler
Photographer: Martin Brigdale
Food Stylist: Valentina Harris
Prop Stylist: Martin Brigdale
Designer: Simon Daley
Illustrator: David Cook
Indexer: Diana LeCore
Proofreading Manager: Lindsay Zamponi
Editorial Reader: Lauren Taylor
Production Controller: Mai-Ling Collyer

NOTES
Bracketed terms are intended for American readers.
For all recipes, quantities are given in both metric and imperial measures and, where appropriate, in standard cups and spoons. Follow one set of measures, but not a mixture, because they are not interchangeable.
• Standard spoon and cup measures are level.
1 tsp = 5ml, 1 tbsp = 15ml, 1 cup = 250ml/8fl oz.
Australian standard tablespoons are 20ml.
Australian readers should use 3 tsp in place of 1 tbsp for measuring small quantities.
• American pints are 16fl oz/2 cups. American readers should use 20fl oz/2.5 cups in place of 1 pint when measuring liquids.
• Electric oven temperatures in this book are for conventional ovens. When using a fan oven, the temperature will probably need to be reduced by about 10–20°C/20–40°F. Since ovens vary, you should check with your manufacturer's instruction book for guidance.
• The nutritional analysis given for each recipe is calculated per portion (i.e. serving or item), unless otherwise stated. If the recipe gives a range, such as Serves 4–6, then the nutritional analysis will be for the smaller portion size, i.e. 6 servings.
The analysis does not include optional ingredients, such as salt added to taste.
• Medium (US large) eggs are used unless otherwise stated.

A CIP catalogue record for this book is available from the British Library.

Front cover shows Sautéed Clams, for recipe see page 75.

ETHICAL TRADING POLICY
At Anness Publishing we believe that business should be conducted in an ethical and ecologically sustainable way, with respect for the environment and a proper regard to the replacement of the natural resources we employ.

As a publisher, we use a lot of wood pulp to make high-quality paper for printing, and that wood commonly comes from spruce trees. We are therefore currently growing more than 750,000 trees in three Scottish forest plantations: Berrymoss (130 hectares/320 acres), West Touxhill (125 hectares/305 acres) and Deveron Forest (75 hectares/185 acres). The forests we manage contain more than 3.5 times the number of trees employed each year in making paper for the books we manufacture.

Because of this ongoing ecological investment programme, you, as our customer, can have the pleasure and reassurance of knowing that a tree is being cultivated on your behalf to naturally replace the materials used to make the book you are holding.

Our forestry programme is run in accordance with the UK Woodland Assurance Scheme (UKWAS) and will be certified by the internationally recognized Forest Stewardship Council (FSC). The FSC is a non-government organization dedicated to promoting responsible management of the world's forests. Certification ensures forests are managed in an environmentally sustainable and socially responsible way. For further information about this scheme, go to www.annesspublishing.com/trees

CONTENTS

A STUNNING LANDSCAPE

The central regions of Italy, comprising Lazio, Campania, Abruzzo and Molise, as well as the charming island of Sardinia, are linked by beautiful countryside and thriving cities. At the very heart of Lazio lies Rome, the Eternal City. With its breathtaking atmosphere, vibrant food culture and diverse population, there is no wonder this ancient city attracts millions of tourists each year. To the south and east, the mountainous Abruzzo and Molise regions have a peaceful agricultural focus. Still further south is Naples, a populous and sprawling metropolis, where many of the best-known Italian dishes were first created. In startling contrast, the lovely island of Sardinia has its own intriguing, unique and well-preserved traditions of food and farming.

ROME AND THE LAZIO REGION

Although the allure of Rome is very strong, Lazio offers an extraordinary variety of landscapes to delight the visitor: wide beaches, pine woods, mountains, gentle hills and expansive plains dotted with picturesque monasteries and ancient villages.

The Lazio region enjoys the typical Mediterranean climate that is characteristic of the western coast of Italy, with hot summers and temperate spring and autumn weather, giving a long growing season that is ideal for farming. Even tender crops such as citrus fruits can be grown in the south of the region, although *la tramontana*, the cold winter wind that blows from the mountains, can cast a chill over the whole area.

Like most regions that were once Papal States, Lazio was historically poor, with little economic development until recent times. Now, however, Lazio contributes 10 per cent of Italy's national wealth from its tourism, agriculture and other key industries.

NAPLES AND THE CAMPANIA REGION

It is hard to begin to describe the extraordinary, chaotic, exciting and resolutely southern city of Naples – it is totally distinct from the rest of Italy. Staunchly Catholic, Naples is rich in historical, artistic and cultural traditions, and has its own distinct cuisine. Pizza, the iconic Italian dish, originated here, and it is eaten, like so many other delicious local foods, out on the street. Neapolitan is a language in its own right and you'll hear the harsh dialect everywhere at full volume. Naples has some beautiful architecture, a thriving port area, and fantastic restaurants and bars serving delicious fresh food.

Running along the gulf of Naples and Sorrento, Campania is home to picturesque towns and strong cultural traditions. The imposing volcano Vesuvius looms on the skyline and the preserved Roman towns of Pompeii and Herculaneum act as a reminder of the damage it caused when it erupted in AD79. The climate is mild, with many hours of sunshine.

BELOW *Lazio, Campania, Abruzzo and Molise make up the heart of mainland Italy, with Sardinia set across the Tyrrhenian Sea.*

BELOW RIGHT *The large, autonomous island of Sardinia is actually set quite far from mainland Italy.*

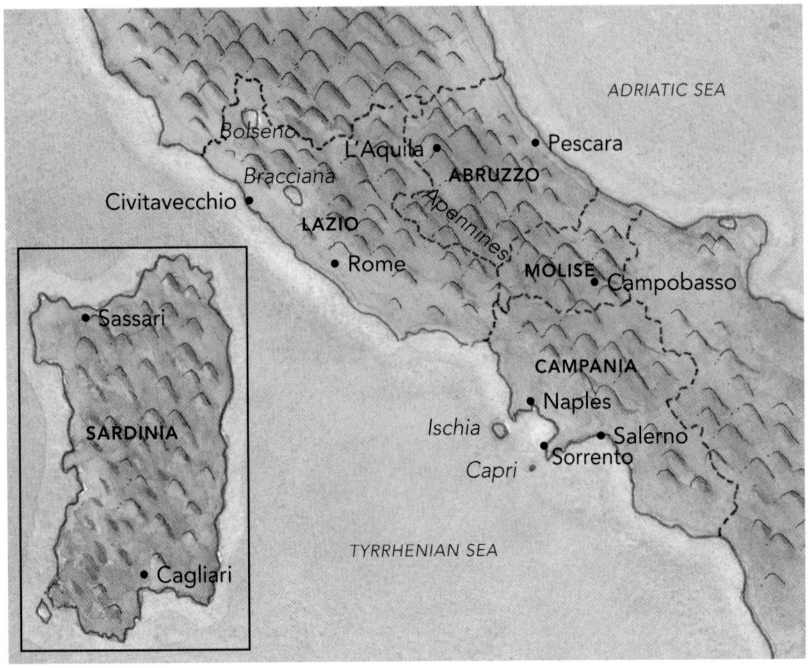

REMOTE ABRUZZO AND MOLISE

The climate of the Abruzzo region is typically Mediterranean near the coast, where the land levels out. However, high up in the Apennines, which dominate the region with their snowy tops, there are very cold winters and hot summers. These high mountains have become popular for walking and skiing. The landscape in the hills and lower mountains is full of green meadows, sparkling rivers and lakes.

The difficult terrain and contrasting temperatures mean that farming is not easy. The hills allow for the cultivation of figs, carrots and grapes, while down on the plains, farmers can grow wheat, potatoes, beetroot (beets) and tobacco. Two rarer specialities of the Abruzzo region are liquorice and saffron, and shepherds tend sheep on the uneven grassy hillsides.

Molise, to the south of Abruzzo, offers some of the most pristine natural areas in all of Europe, with fragrant green forests, expansive plains and snow-topped mountains. Nestling in the landscape are well-preserved medieval castles and hamlets, and fascinating ancient ruins that date back to the 4th century BC.

A BEAUTIFUL COASTLINE

The beauty of Campania has always caught the attention of artists and poets. During the times of the ancient Greeks, Campania was home to Homer's sirens. Later, during the Roman period, the region was a hot spot among the rich, who built breathtaking villas by the sea. The Amalfi Coast, claimed by many to be the most beautiful stretch of coastline in Europe, has lemon groves sloping down to the blue sea, with brightly coloured houses climbing the hillside.

THE RUGGED ISLAND OF SARDINIA

The second largest island in the Mediterranean Sea (after Sicily), Sardinia is hot and dry in summer, while spring and autumn are pleasant. Winters are mild and humid with the occasional hot day. The island is surrounded by the warm Mediterranean and its long coastline sees plenty of sun. The terrain is not easy for farmers, with high hills and mountains inland. Agriculture tends to focus on livestock and growing tender crops, such as olives, citrus fruits and grapes. Fish is also plentiful in the surrounding waters and forms an important part of the diet.

Sardinia is one of two Italian regions whose inhabitants have been recognized as a *popolo* (a distinct people) by a local statute; the other region is the Veneto. The people here, unusually, have more in common genetically with Bosnia and Croatia than they do with the rest of Italy.

ABOVE LEFT *A shepherd leads his flock over the mountain grasslands of Campo Imperatore in the L'Aquila province of Abruzzo.*

ABOVE *Sardinia's long, picturesque coastline surrounds a rugged and mountainous interior.*

BELOW *The bustling metropolis of Naples sprawls along the beautiful Campania coastline, with Mount Vesuvius looming on the horizon.*

A POWERFUL HISTORY

The central regions of Italy have a colourful history that dates as far back as the Bronze Age, if not further. From the legend of Romulus and Remus to the spread of the Roman Empire, the story of central Italy, with Rome at the heart, is universally known. The influence of this glorious city was felt not only in the surrounding area of what is now Italy, but also far and wide across the world due to the spread of the all-powerful Roman Empire. After the decline of the Roman Empire, the whole region was controlled by various powers, which led to many new dishes and ingredients being incorporated into the local cuisine. Sardinia's isolated position has created a unique history, which is illustrated in its architecture and food culture.

BELOW *Rome displays a wealth of fabulously preserved architecture and art from many periods of history, such as the awe-inspiring St. Peter's Basilica at the heart of Vatican City.*

ROME AND LAZIO: A CENTRE OF POWER

The founding of Rome goes back to the very early days of civilization. Kings first governed Rome, but after a short time, the citizens took power over their own city and ruled themselves for nearly 500 years, followed by the Roman Empire under many different emperors for a further 500 years. Roman food and drink were a most important aspect of the culture, which was exported across the globe.

The Roman Empire had collapsed by the year AD476. In the succeeding years, invaders came and went, leaving behind their own artistic and culinary traditions, and the fabric of Rome was left in very poor shape. Gradually Roman pride reasserted itself, but it was not until the 19th century that the structure of modern Italy, with Rome as the capital, was fully established. Some of the world's most important art and architecture resides here, and Rome also contains Vatican City, a city-state and the centre of the Catholic Church, within its boundaries.

The region that is now known as Lazio, right in the centre of Italy, has been home to agricultural populations since the early Bronze Age. People settled in this pleasant, equable climate, raising crops and keeping animals for food. From the Middle Ages to the 18th century, Lazio served as an important centre for all forms of artistic and scientific creation and development, keeping the flame of culture alive through multiple invasions. Its decline in the lean years of the 18th and 19th centuries has been reversed at last, and in the 21st century, mainly because of successful Rome, Lazio has regained its reputation as a forward-thinking area with plenty of entrepreneurial spirit.

NAPLES AND CAMPANIA: GRECO-ROMAN UNITY

The bustling, energetic, sometimes lawless city of Naples is still regarded as the capital of the south of Italy. Naples was probably founded by the Greeks in the 8th century BC, a few kilometres from the older town of Partenope, when Campania was part of the Magna Græcia. This new town or 'neapolis' (from where it got its name) has been absorbing the influences of its settlers and invaders ever since.

Campania was part of the Roman Empire by the 4th century AD, although its inhabitants still spoke Greek; it was a centre of Greco-Roman culture. Its fertile landscape and elegant Greek architecture made it an important and respected region. Campania changed hands many times in the next few centuries, and became part of Italy as we know it in October 1860.

Today, Naples is most famous for its rich, simple dishes that have transcended international borders, including the basic pizza, made of just a few ingredients, but of very good quality.

ABRUZZO AND MOLISE

Many different tribes populated this part of Italy in ancient times, living a predominantly pastoral life, caring for their animals and growing food. People inhabited the few low-lying areas along the Adriatic seashore and beside the rivers in the green, fertile valleys. During the Augustan era (27BC to AD14), the whole region was finally subdued and incorporated into the Roman Empire, after much fierce resistance from the local people.

Between the 6th and 19th centuries, the region underwent numerous changes of government due to its position as a wedge between the north and south of Italy. Garibaldi's campaign to unify Italy brought all the regions together in 1860, but this was no unqualified blessing – Molise and Abruzzo suffered from their relatively poor development during the centuries of constant fighting, and there was a spate of migration, both abroad and to other parts of the country. It was not until 1963 that Molise was recognized as a separate region from Abruzzo, with its own proud, age-old traditions.

LEFT *A farmer in Sardinia travels on a donkey across the terrain, a reminder of the peasant agricultural traditions that have existed on the island for centuries.*

SARDINIA: AN ANCIENT LAND

The island dates back to the Cambrian period, 570 million years ago. With the periodic fluctuation of sea level, Sardinia has at times been linked physically to the rest of Italy, and people and animals crossed the land bridge to and from Tuscany.

The scant population that lived in Sardinia from around 1800BC to 200BC built the strange conical towers that are still a characteristic feature of the rugged Sardinian landscape. This population was mainly a pastoral people and their basic traditions of farming, using the same simple methods, have been maintained in Sardinia for over 3,000 years, right up to the present day. It is still common to see peasant farmers travelling around by donkey and, up to just a few years ago, you could occasionally witness the tilling of the land with an ox-drawn wooden plough.

Throughout its history, Sardinia fell prey to invaders and marauders, due to its position in the middle of the Mediterranean Sea. It is no wonder, therefore, that most of the main cities are set inland, and well protected. The highest mountain peak, Monte Moro, is so called because it provided a lookout against the Moors. On the coast, older cottages are tucked away where they could not be seen from the sea. Moreover, Sardinia lacks a fishing history – the sea was a dangerous place – and today's fishermen tend to be descendants of migrants from the Pontine Islands, close to the mainland.

BELOW LEFT *The Greco-Roman temple at Paestum in Campania was built by the Greeks in about 500BC.*

BELOW RIGHT *Abruzzo and Molise have retained a largely pastoral landscape and a strong history of farming.*

A WORLD-FAMOUS CUISINE

To many people outside of Italy, 'Italian cuisine' is basically Neapolitan cooking. This is partly because many of the Italian immigrants all around the world came from the city of Naples and its environs. When these ambitious migrants opened restaurants in their new countries, they naturally served the style of food they loved and knew best: the cooking of Naples and Campania. However, there is much more to the central region than Naples. Lazio, Abruzzo, Molise and the island of Sardinia all have their own traditions of making delicious dishes using local ingredients, including tender lamb from the sheep trails of Abruzzo, fresh fish from the Campania coastline, gutsy pasta sauces and offal from Rome, and speciality Sardinian desserts.

THE CUISINE OF ROME AND LAZIO

Traditional cooking in Lazio reflects the simple, sustaining meals of shepherds and farmers. It's no surprise that tender, milk-fed lamb is a favourite dish, usually roasted and served with seasonal vegetables. The cuisine is a savoury tapestry, incorporating the farming traditions of the region with an amalgam of ingredients from outlying areas, including Umbria. The vegetables found in the markets are of exceptional quality, perhaps because of the sun-drenched volcanic soil of the region.

Fish is an integral part of Roman cuisine, and features most frequently in Rome as salt cod – baccalà. Offal is also key, and although it has been ousted from many of the more refined city-centre

ROMAN PASTA

Although all sorts of pasta shapes are served in Roman restaurants, spaghetti and the local specialities bucatini or tonnarelli (thick-cut spaghetti) are the favourite shapes. These chunky strips of pasta stand up well to the coarse, rich sauces the Romans prefer, such as a very simple, strong-tasting aglio e olio (garlic and oil), cacio e pepe (Pecorino cheese and ground black pepper), alla carbonara (with beaten eggs, cubes of pan-fried pork or bacon, and Pecorino or Parmesan cheese), and alle vongole (with fresh baby clams).

BELOW *A store in Naples sells dried durum wheat pasta in a multitude of shapes and sizes.*

BELOW RIGHT *The market of Campo de Fiori in Rome is awash with the vibrant colours of fresh fruit and vegetables each day.*

restaurants, it still appears on the menus of more traditional eateries, especially those in the Testaccio area. More conventional meat dishes include abbacchio (milk-fed lamb roasted to melting tenderness with rosemary, sage and garlic), scottadito (grilled lamb chops eaten with the fingers) and saltimbocca alla romana (thin slices of veal cooked with a slice of prosciutto, mozzarella cheese and sage on top). Artichokes are the quintessential Roman vegetable, served alla Romana (stuffed with garlic and mint) and in all their unadulterated glory, alla Giudia (flattened and fried in olive oil, Jewish-style).

No description of the gastronomy of Rome would be complete without a mention of the city's countless bars, cafés and restaurants, where Romans can be found morning, noon and night, sipping their daily cappuccinos, or eating and drinking with family and friends.

NEAPOLITAN STREET FOOD

Food in Naples is a joyful experience, always to be shared with friends and family. There are all kinds of fast foods available, from friggi e mangia ('fry and eat'), or the products of the local rosticceria (delicatessen), to various passatempi ('fill-time'), little treats of shellfish, small pizzas, tarts or fritters which are offered at kiosks and street stalls and are eaten at any hungry moment throughout the day. In these traditional foods, Naples extravagantly displays its legendary culinary heritage for all to admire.

NAPLES AND THE CAMPANIA REGION

This is a region in which both peasant and noble cuisines have grown up alongside each other, using the same produce. Superb fruits and vegetables are grown here, particularly tomatoes and aubergines (eggplants). Other favourite ingredients include the mild mozzarella cheese that is made from water buffalo milk, which is often served with tomatoes as a salad called la Caprese.

As in Rome, the most common pasta shape is spaghetti, frequently served with shellfish and meatless marinara tomato sauce. Fish and shellfish are brought in from the Mediterranean as a principal protein source and they are far more widely eaten than red meat, which is usually reserved for major feast days.

The pizza, the most famous creation of Neapolitan cuisine, is one of the most representative dishes of Naples. Resplendent with its tomato topping, sizzling and cheerful, pizza became extremely popular amongst the masses in the 18th century, but also with barons and princes: it was a main feature at the grand receptions of the Bourbons. The pizza-maker Raffaele Esposito created a patriotic tri-colour pizza for Queen Margherita of Savoie in 1889. The three colours of the Italian flag, white, red and green, became a topping of mozzarella, tomato and basil.

ABOVE LEFT *Pizza remains the iconic Neapolitan dish and is cooked and eaten with delight throughout the city.*

ABOVE *Coffees and other drinks are enjoyed outside a café on the famous Via Veneto in 1950s Rome, a typically Roman scene that has hardly changed to this day.*

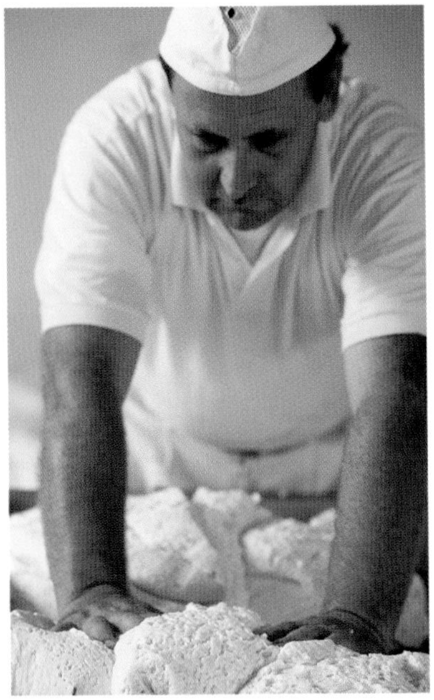

ABOVE *Creamy buffalo mozzarella is made by hand in Campania.*

ABOVE RIGHT *Young factory workers in the 1930s carry spaghetti out to dry in a factory yard in Naples.*

There are numerous varieties of pizza, including quattro formaggi (four cheeses), frutti di mare (shellfish), and alla marinara (tomato and garlic), but the presence of tomato, at least in Naples, is guaranteed.

Other glories of Neapolitan cuisine include recipes based on the magnificent vegetables of the Campania countryside, such as parmigiana di melanzane (aubergines baked with tomato and cheese) or stuffed sweet peppers. The fruits of the sea feature in many classic dishes, such as polpi alla Luciana (octopus Luciana style), which originates from the working class quarter of Santa Lucia; it is cooked with hot chilli peppers and the ever-present tomatoes. Dairy products, particularly cheeses such as provolone, scamorza, caciocavallo and ricotta, are also an important part of Neapolitan cuisine. The queen of the cheeses, however, is mozzarella, a fresh, soft, white cheese with a stringy texture, made from buffalo milk.

Pasta was not invented in Naples, but here it has certainly reached the highest levels of perfection. Local pasta dishes are extraordinary for the care with which the pasta is cooked – it must be al dente. From the classic simple pummarola (tomato sauce), through a whole range of more elaborate sauces based on vegetables or shellfish, right up to the apotheosis of slow-cooked ragù meat sauce, the creativity of the area is in real evidence in pasta dishes.

The cakes and desserts of Naples are a delicious, rich treat: ice creams, babas, spumoni, sfogliatelle, taralli and the magnificent pastiera, the cake eaten from Epiphany to Easter, made with ricotta cheese, orange flower water, cinnamon and candied fruit.

TOMATOES

At the heart of Neapolitan cuisine there is an ingredient which merits a mention in its own right: the tomato. It was brought to Italy from South America in the 16th century, but it was only around the beginning of the 19th century that it became a common ingredient in many Italian recipes. It is now one of the most important and iconic of all the crops grown in Campania.

THE CUISINE OF ABRUZZO AND MOLISE

Rugged mountains (the highest peaks in the Apennines), palm-lined beaches and charming hill towns combine to make Abruzzo one of Italy's most beautiful and geographically diverse regions. It is a place where ancient agricultural traditions are still handed down from one generation to the next. The region is famous for its livestock production and farming, including crops of the highly prized spice saffron, and for the fish and shellfish caught along the coast of the Adriatic Sea.

Pasta, vegetables and meat (especially lamb and pork) are the staples of Abruzzo cuisine. Many lamb dishes and subtly aromatic cheeses, such as Pecorino (from sheep's milk) and scamorza (from cow's milk, often smoked), are rooted in pasture farming and the everyday life of the region's shepherds, although their numbers are now in decline. The legendary panarda, a colossal thanksgiving banquet of up to 30 courses that dates back hundreds of years, and is still occasionally held today, is symbolic of the region's devotion to good eating.

Very little meat is eaten in Molise, a result of a tradition called *la transumanza*, when the townspeople walked their sheep to Puglia to be sold. Because people were travelling a lot, many Molisani dishes reflect simplicity and a quick preparation time, and meat was considered a luxury. Today in Molise, vegetables and cheese dominate, along with pasta, grains and fresh fruits. Like their neighbours in Abruzzo, the people of Molise love the hot chilli pepper, affectionately known as diavolino, or little devil, adding it to nearly every savoury dish.

THE ANCIENT TRADITIONS OF SARDINIA

Sardinian cuisine is a celebration of products from the land and surrounding sea. The flavours of the natural ingredients are enriched by the unmistakable aromas of the island's Mediterranean herbs and plants. This cuisine is strictly linked to the seasons and its secret lies in the quality of the ingredients and the simplicity of its dishes. It offers up a triumph of unique tastes, with each area boasting a vast selection of local specialities, which are all prepared according to ancient traditions and customs.

Among the many celebrated meat dishes, the most well-known is unquestionably porceddu (suckling pig cooked on a spit or in a hole dug in the ground, using the aromatic wood of the Mediterranean scrubland). However, there are numerous other mouthwatering meat dishes, such as rabbit a succhittu, served in a sauce made from the rabbit's liver, wine, capers and tomatoes; wild boar in Cannonau wine; or chicken wrapped in myrtle leaves. Fish dishes also abound on the island, with hundreds of recipes for all kinds of fish and shellfish. Bottarga (salted or dried mullet or tuna eggs) is a favourite all along the south-west coast of the island and is often considered to be the caviar of Sardinia.

Sardinian desserts are justly famous throughout Italy. Round, sweet ravioli called sebardas, filled with cheese, are fried and then covered in sweet, sticky honey. Also popular are the special biscuits (cookies) known as sospiri, which translates as 'sighs', as well as nougat and other confections made from almonds and sweet cheeses.

SARDINIAN BREAD

The Romans called Sardinia 'the granary of Rome', and the local wheat and flour means there is a rich selection of bread, pasta and desserts. Each region boasts its own bread, made with special techniques according to ancient recipes. One of the most famous of these is pane carasau, wafer-thin sheets of toasted bread, also known as carta da musica (music paper). This bread is typical of the Barbagia region and was a staple part of the shepherds' diet.

BELOW LEFT *Local women collect crocus flowers in Abruzzo, ready to prepare the highly-prized saffron.*

BELOW *A variety of local breads have been typically made by hand in Sardinia for centuries.*

FESTIVALS AND CELEBRATIONS

Many regions of Italy maintain the generations-old tradition of putting on local festivals to celebrate not only religious holidays but also the arrival of the new season's crops. It is a matter of pride, particularly in this agricultural central area of Italy, that a rich vegetable harvest, a prolific haul from the sea or the careful husbandry of animals for meat or dairy products should be celebrated with a feast. Festivals bring whole villages or towns together, year after year, with traditional rituals, songs and dancing, as well as a wealth of regional foods being cooked and served to festival-goers. The Italians love an excuse for a party, and from the large religious ceremonies to the smallest, most unusual festivals, these celebrations are well worth a visit.

FESTIVALS OF LAZIO AND ROME

In April, the Matticella Artichoke Festival in Velletri uses the matticelle, the long vine shoots that are kept and left to dry after the vines have been pruned, to fuel the fires for cooking artichokes, which are served to everyone who passes by.

Summer festivals in Lazio include the Laina e Fasuri Festival in Sant'Ambrogio sul Garigliano – only in Italy would a simple dish of home-made pasta served with beans qualify for its own festival. It is eaten by everyone in the town at this time of year. Another local speciality is enjoyed at the Marzoline Festival in Esperia in August, which celebrates a goat's milk cheese made in the mountains of the Monti Aurinci Natural Park. Tradition demands that it is left to mature for a few days on wooden racks and then aged for several months in glass jars.

FESTIVALS OF NAPLES AND CAMPANIA

In early summer, at the Lemon Festival at Massa Lubrense, the local crop of these special lemons is celebrated with a delightful festival of food and fun. Here you can sample the classic Caprese salad with lemon, or for a sweet treat, lemon ice cream and lemon granita. This is also the place for a glass of the famous Limoncello in its area of origin.

The PizzaFest in Naples takes pride of place in September. This world-famous Neapolitan dish stars at PizzaFest, and the visitor can taste pizzas of many different types and shapes, as well as other Neapolitan foods. There is a feast for the eyes and ears too, as pizza makers show off their dough-throwing skills and everyone dances to live music.

At Christmas in Naples, the Christmas markets in the Spanish Quarter burst into life. Although the main focus is the delightfully carved Christmas nativity scenes, or presepi, stallholders will not lose the opportunity to sell hot snacks to the passerby, such as individual pizzas or deep-fried slices of aubergine (eggplant).

CHRISTMAS IN ROME

In November and December, the Piazza Navona Christmas market takes place in this spectacular square in Rome, and runs right through to Twelfth Night, when La Befana, the Christmas witch, calls to bring presents to the children. Christmas cribs and other decorations glow alongside stalls selling sweets, chestnuts, sugared apples, the famous torrone (nougat) and liquorice.

FESTIVALS OF ABRUZZO AND MOLISE

Spring festivals in Molise include the Scurpelle Festival in Fossalto, which celebrates this local speciality, a kind of savoury fritter made with flour, eggs, salt and yeast, and fried in very hot oil.

The Scattone Festival in Gildone in August focuses on a special kind of pasta dough, cooked in boiling water to which wine is added according to taste, with a spoonful of sugar, a pinch of peppercorns or crushed chilli pepper. Apparently, this fierce, hot pasta dish is very good for curing colds.

BELOW *Chestnuts are roasted on the streets of Rome during the Christmas period.*

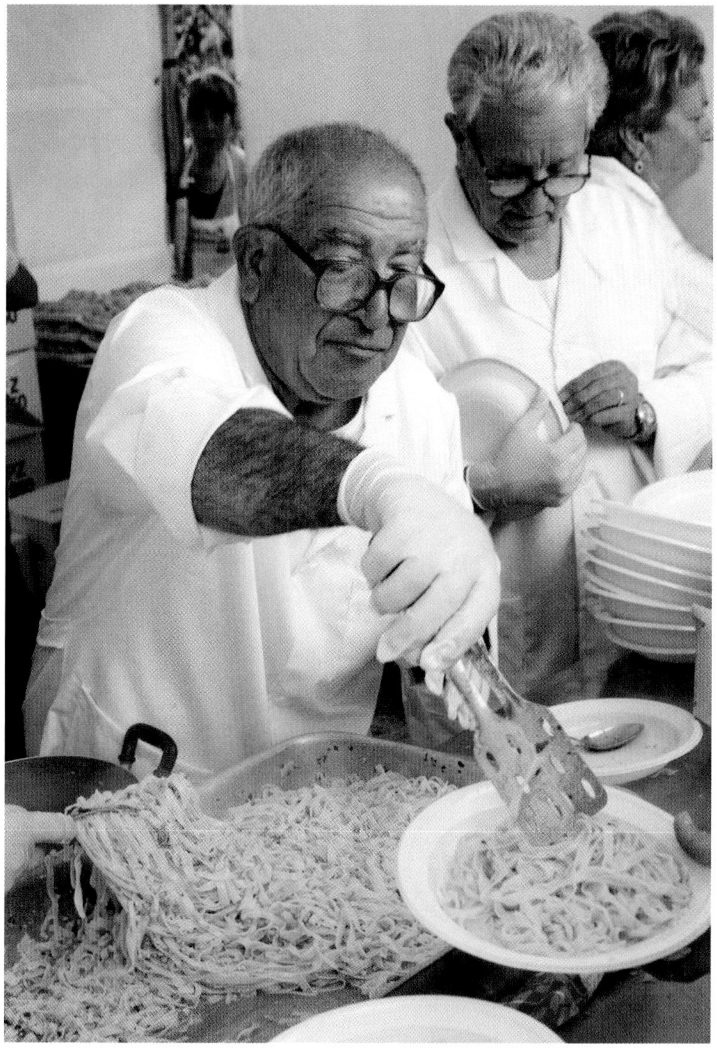

ABOVE LEFT *Pasta, the iconic Italian food, is served at a festival in the tiny town of Accumoli in Lazio.*

ABOVE *PizzaFest takes place each year in Naples, where the age-old tradition of pizza-making is celebrated with fabulous displays of dough-spinning and a vast array of toppings.*

FESTIVALS OF SARDINIA

In early spring, the Sardinian carnival season, with its strange and ancient rituals, starts on the night of the feast of Sant'Antonio Abate in January, with bonfires lighting up towns and villages. In the Barbagia region the carnival unfolds with processions made up of people in sombre masks, who move with rhythmical step to the haunting sound of bells, recalling ancient rural rites.

The important religious festival of Easter is celebrated with numerous solemn ceremonies. In Castelsardo, all the people of the town join together for a meal at lunchtime, before a candlelit procession and chanting choirs lead the way round the town in the dark.

Summer brings more food-related festivals in Sardinia. In June, the remote rural area of Meana Sardo, in the centre of Sardinia, celebrates the local sheep's cheese, Pecorino, and other local dairy products. This Pecorino cheese tastes delicious grilled and spread on thin toasted sheets of Sardinian bread, pane carasau.

The Honey Festival of Montevecchio is held in the Geo-Mineral Sardinian Park, an area that is well suited to the production of arbutus blossom honey. And in September, the Su Succu Festival at Busachi makes a centrepiece of the local recipe for angel-hair noodles dropped into a delicious meat soup.

A GRAND REUNION

The International Chefs' Festival takes place every year at Sangro in Abruzzo on the second Sunday of October. The Val di Sangro, a mountain valley in the province of Chieti, is renowned for producing generations of chefs who have turned Abruzzo's simple yet sophisticated regional foods into culinary wonders. In celebration, this festival draws chefs home from all over the world to share their expertise and sample the delicacies of local restaurants from special stands lined up along the village's main street.

CLASSIC INGREDIENTS

The best Italian cuisine is always based on the freshest possible local produce. In the chilly north, root vegetables and warming stews predominate; in the hot south, citrus fruits, grapes and olives take centre stage. In this central region, with its two bustling cosmopolitan cities and its fascinating history, a wonderful cuisine has developed, based on the ingredients that thrive here: tomatoes, artichokes, lemons and durum wheat from the fields, sheep's cheese and meat from the hillsides, and fresh fish and shellfish from the sea. Local, seasonal, fresh produce is key to the success of the regional cuisine, and Italian chefs always focus on using the best-quality basic ingredients in their cooking.

VEGETABLES

The fertile soil and benign climate of central Italy makes it an ideal spot to grow all kinds of vegetables. By far the biggest crop is tomatoes, which were brought to central Italy after the conquest of South America in the 16th century and are now a feature of hundreds of recipes from the region. The flavour of sun-ripened tomatoes grown naturally in the open air is quite outstanding.

One of the simplest and most refreshing tomato recipes is from Positano, a hill village in the region of Campania. Here, hot pasta is dressed with a 'seven-flavour' sauce of cold chopped tomatoes dressed with basil, oregano, parsley, chopped onion, celery, garlic and olive oil. So many savoury dishes from Rome and Naples include tomatoes that it would almost be quicker to list those that do not.

ROMAN ARTICHOKES

Artichokes are enormously popular in Italy, where some 90 different varieties are grown, and they are especially prized in Rome.

They are flattened and fried twice for the simple but tasty dish, carciofi alla Giudia (artichokes Jewish style), an ancient recipe that originates from the Roman ghetto. Another favourite dish from the capital city is known as carciofi alla Romana – artichokes stuffed with mint, lemon and garlic.

Local farmers and gardeners grow all kinds of other vegetables, including courgettes (zucchini), lentils, potatoes, cannellini beans, (bell) peppers,

BELOW, LEFT TO RIGHT
Aubergines, yellow peppers and tomatoes.

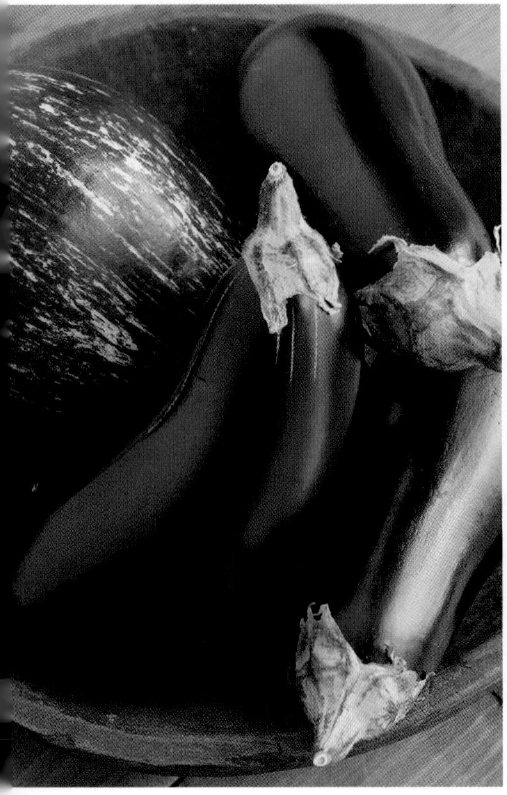

broad (fava) beans and aubergines (eggplants). These crop up in many salads and other side dishes, but the main focus in the central region of Italy is always on the tomato, which reigns supreme.

FRUIT AND NUTS

Lemons and oranges grow well in the south of central Italy, both around Naples and further east, in the Molise region. Here the climate is reliably warm all year round, and the fruit receives plenty of sunlight. The Sorrento ovale, also known as the Massa Lubrense lemon, is a high quality, strongly perfumed medium-to-large lemon that is identified by its sweet, juicy flesh and few pips (seeds). Even its cultivation is special: the precious fruit is hand-picked to prevent it falling to the ground, and is ripened under pagliarelle, straw mats attached to wooden poles (preferably made of chestnut wood), which help to protect the plants.

Orchard fruits such as apples and pears are also grown here. In the inland parts of Molise, well away from the Adriatic coast, you can still find orchards with an old type of apple tree that produces very aromatic fruit called mela limoncella. They have a green-yellow skin and a slightly acidic, sweet flavour.

DAIRY PRODUCE

Beautiful fragrant soft cheeses abound in central Italy, and are used in many recipes, either as a topping or melted into a sauce. Mozzarella di bufala campana, or buffalo mozzarella, is the most celebrated and highly prized of mozzarella cheeses, made exclusively from whole buffalo milk. It is indispensable for classics such as the Caprese salad. Similar cheeses include scamorza (a kind of smoked mozzarella from cow's milk), mateca, provatura and burrino.

A harder, sharper-tasting cheese made of sheep's milk is known as Pecorino. This tasty, strong cheese can be used in a similar way to the better-known Parmesan, sprinkled on top of pasta dishes or soups.

Soft cheeses such as ricotta and cream cheese also feature in many recipes such as calzone, a folded pizza where the soft cheese is spread over the dough before the other topping ingredients. A firm ricotta is sometimes used as part of a fritto misto, an Italian kind of fry-up based on mixed fish and shellfish and chunks of cheese fried in batter.

EGGS

Many people still keep chickens in their gardens and use them for both eggs and meat. Eggs can be a main ingredient in a delicious appetizer such as Roman egg and cheese soup or deep-fried mozzarella sandwiches, and are an integral part of the famous dish, spaghetti carbonara.

BELOW, LEFT TO RIGHT *Pecorino, ricotta and scamorza.*

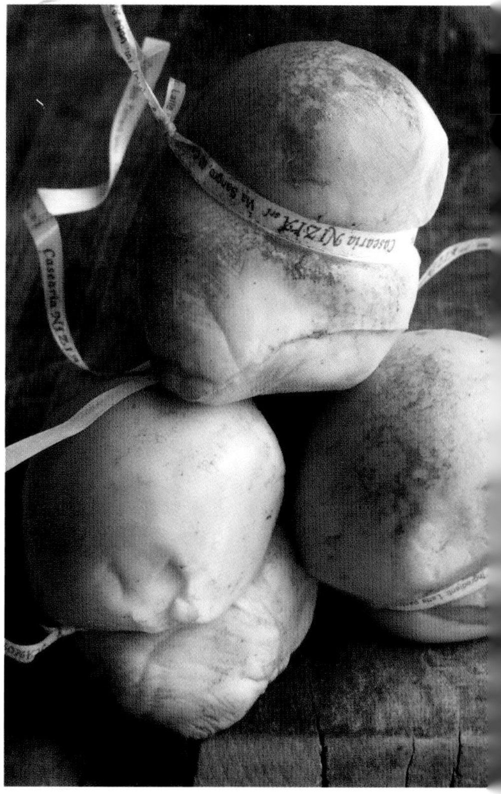

ABOVE, LEFT TO RIGHT
Pancetta, salami, anchovies and prawns, and clams.

MEAT AND POULTRY

The cuisine of these regions of Italy does not rely to a great extent on meat. Even where sheep are bred, such as in the hilly Molise region, they are often exported to other Italian regions to be sold rather than being eaten locally. Chicken is perhaps the most common meat, and every bit of the bird is used, whether it's in the form of a roast main course or a soup from the carcass.

The same thrifty attitude prevails in many other meat recipes. Every part of the animal, including the offal, can be turned into a tasty dish with a little care. Preserving pork in the form of prosciutto (air-dried ham), pancetta (salted, spiced bacon) or sausage was the traditional way to eke out the meat supply over the winter. Fresh meat usually takes the form of lamb, pork and veal stews; beef is a real rarity on the menu.

FISH AND SHELLFISH

All sorts of delicious fish and shellfish dishes are made in this land surrounded by sea. The fish cooked here is often whitebait or sea bass, or a meaty tuna steak. Shellfish such as clams, squid, prawns (shrimp) or mussels predominate, often bathed in a tasty, salty pasta sauce.

Fish roe (bottarga), also known as Sardinian caviar, is considered one of the most authentic, flavoursome examples of the island's gastronomic tradition. It is often served on top of pasta, or in fine slices, alongside pieces of celery drizzled with good olive oil, or combined with artichoke hearts, uniting two classic Sardinian products from the land and sea.

BREAD AND PIZZA

The classic breads of Sardinia tend to be hard and dry, and they are prepared only once a week rather than every day as in many other European countries. Pane carasau, a crisp, very thin bread that is made from durum wheat semolina and wheat flour, can keep for weeks owing to its very low water content; traditionally, it was the kind of bread that shepherds carried with them to the high mountain pastures. On the mainland, bread tends to be white and soft, and is at its best when it is eaten fresh.

Pizza is often thought of as the most typical Italian food by non-Italians, but outside Naples, it was hardly known until the 1970s. Today pizza is enormously popular all over the world, even if it sometimes hardly resembles the original dish. In the classic Neapolitan pizza, only three versions are permitted: Marinara, with tomatoes, garlic and oregano; Margherita, with basil, tomatoes and mozzarella; and Extra Margherita, which must always include buffalo mozzarella from the Campania region.

PASTA, POLENTA AND RICE

Some of Italy's best-known pasta dishes originated in Lazio. Romans, whose passion for pasta is legendary, take credit for inventing spaghetti alla puttanesca ('streetwalker's spaghetti', so named for the local prostitutes who were said to enjoy its nourishing qualities), and spaghetti alla carbonara, made with bacon, eggs, butter and cheese.

The quintessential pasta of Sardinia is malloreddus, a small gnocchi made from durum wheat semolina, salt and water, and given its distinctive yellow colour by the addition of saffron. Pieces of the pasta dough are rolled across thin wires or a board to give them their characteristic ridged surface. Malloreddus are traditionally served with a simple tomato sauce, a hearty lamb or sausage ragù, or just with butter and grated Pecorino cheese.

Because of their joint history, Molise shares many of the culinary traditions of Abruzzo, and there are few dishes unique to the region. One that does stand out is polenta d'iragn, a white polenta made with potatoes and wheat and served with a tomato sauce.

Maccheroni alla chitarra from the Abruzzo region is an egg pasta that is made with a chitarra, a rectangular beechwood frame over which fine metal strings are stretched, like those on a guitar. The thinly rolled pasta dough is laid over the strings

BASIC PIZZA DOUGH

MAKES 6 SINGLE PORTION PIZZAS OR FOCACCIAS

25g/1oz fresh yeast
200ml/7fl oz warm water
pinch sugar
2.5ml/½ tsp sea salt
400g/14oz strong white bread flour
10–15ml/2–3 tsp olive oill

1 Mix the yeast and water together with the sugar and salt, and add about 30ml/2 tbsp of the flour. Put the yeast mixture in a lightly floured bowl and place it somewhere warm to rise for about 10–20 minutes.

2 Place the rest of the flour in a mound on a clean work surface. Stir the yeast mixture thoroughly, and then knead it into the rest of the flour, adding more water if required to make a soft dough.

3 Add the salt and the oil. Knead energetically together for 10–20 minutes. The dough should stretch to a length of about 25cm/10in without snapping.

4 Transfer this mixture to a large floured bowl and return to a warm place to rise again for about 1 hour or until it has doubled in size.

5 Use as required in the recipe. Alternatively, roll it out into rounds, spread with passata (bottled strained tomatoes), then sprinkle with toppings, such as garlic, oregano, basil and cheese. Bake for 5–10 minutes at 220°C/425°C/Gas 7.

and pushed through with a rolling pin, cutting it into uniformly fine strands. Traditionally, the maccheroni is served with a lamb, tomato and peperoncino sauce, sprinkled with the local Pecorino cheese.

SPICES, HERBS AND FLAVOURINGS

Olives crop up in a variety of recipes. Whole olives are used for pasta and pizza toppings and sprinkled into a salad, while olive oil is used in almost every savoury recipe as the cooking oil of choice. Fragrant olive oil can also be found as the main ingredient in the most basic pasta dressing of all, aglio e olio (garlic and olive oil). Butter is reserved for frying delicate fish or blending into cakes and pastries.

A single garlic clove helps release the savoury taste of many a tomato-based sauce, but this pungent bulb comes into its own in such dishes as the above-mentioned aglio e olio, as well as in lamb recipes, where its strong flavour stands up to the equally strong taste of anchovies and vinegar in Roman roast lamb.

The local herbs are basil, which blends so well with tomatoes, as well as sage, parsley and oregano. Juniper berries bring their sharp, distinctive flavour to braised dishes such as a hearty chicken stew, while capers brighten up a side dish based on yellow peppers, or the fiery pasta sauce, puttanesca.

IL DIAVOLINO

The red chilli pepper, known to the people of Abruzzo as diavolino (little devil), is a key ingredient in the local cuisine. It spices up everything from brodetto alla Pescarese, a fish soup made in the fishing port city of Pescara, to a dish of tagliolini pasta with ham from Molise.

SWEET THINGS

There are many wonderfully creamy, light recipes for desserts that round off a good meal. Many of them are based on cream cheese, crystallized fruit and nuts, spiced with cinnamon or vanilla. Tiramisù, which means 'pick me up', may not have originated in Rome, but it is an adopted speciality of the city. The ingredients – mascarpone, eggs, sugar, espresso coffee, boudoir biscuits, a sweet liqueur and cocoa – result in an absolutely scrumptious cold dessert.

Parrozzo is another famous local dessert from the Abruzzo region: this is a soft cake made with flour, butter, eggs, sugar and almonds, covered with chocolate. La pastiera, a traditional cake for Easter from Naples, is an interesting mixture of ricotta cheese and cooked wheat grains with candied peel, sugar and eggs, baked in a pastry shell.

BELOW, LEFT TO RIGHT
Flat leaf parsley, dried oregano, pine nuts and Limoncello.

DRINKS

Wine is a part of daily life in the central part of Italy, as it is in most other regions of this grape-growing country, and a glass of wine is added to many hearty meat stews and tasty pasta sauces. Local wines vary from those exclusively drunk locally to those that are exported all round the world, such as Frascati from Lazio. Sardinia produces many fine wines, which are, however, quite hard to find on sale elsewhere.

Other alcoholic drinks include Cent'erbe, which is the most powerful of all Italian liqueurs. Emerald green in colour, with a high alcohol content, it was first produced by herbalists from various plants indigenous to the mountains of Abruzzo, and was sold as a cure for the plague during the epidemic in the late 1600s.

Also worth remembering are the two famous digestifs from Sardinia: Mirto, made from the wild myrtle which grows so profusely, and Filu Ferru, the much harsher, pure white spirit, the local version of grappa.

One of Italy most well-known drinks is a product made from Sorrento lemons. Called Limoncello (or limunciel, as the Campanians call it), it is a delicious liqueur that is the result of an infusion of lemon peel in the purest alcohol. It goes into many desserts, including cakes and ice cream, and is drunk on its own as well.

TOMATO SAUCE

SERVES 6

1 onion
1 large carrot
1 large celery stick
60ml/4 tbsp extra virgin olive oil
500g/1¼lb fresh or canned tomatoes or passata (bottled strained tomatoes)
sea salt and freshly ground black pepper

1 Peel and chop the onion very finely. Scrape and wash the carrot, then chop finely. Finally, wash the celery, tear away the strings and then chop finely; a few celery leaves would also be welcome.

2 Pour the oil into a large, heavy pan and add all the chopped vegetables. Fry very gently for about 10 minutes, until the vegetables are soft and the onion becomes transparent. This is known as a soffritto.

3 Add the tomatoes and stir thoroughly.

4 Cover and leave to simmer for about 30 minutes, stirring regularly. Season to taste and use as required in a recipe, or serve over pasta. If you wish to add fresh herbs, do so at the end once the sauce is cooked.

SOUPS AND ANTIPASTI

ZUPPE, MINESTRE E ANTIPASTI

The best way to describe the style of cooking and presentation that is shared by the recipes presented in this chapter, and indeed throughout the book, is that they tend to be satisfyingly robust and hearty. Sardinian food is perhaps an exception, but overall the liberal use of flavoursome ingredients such as garlic, chilli, oregano and basil gives many of these dishes a full-bodied identity. The soups are rich and tasty, and the appetizers are unusually sustaining. Cheeses feature prominently here, sprinkled over soups, served in salads, toasted or stuffed in deep-fried treats. Mozzarella abounds in the appetizers of central Italy and Sardinia, as do the tasty Roman provatura and Pecorino.

FRESH BASIL, TOMATOES AND MOZZARELLA

One of Campania's (and Italy's) most famous and best-loved ingredients is, of course, mozzarella, which is used to prepare countless antipasti dishes, such as Tomato, Basil and Mozzarella Salad, known as la Caprese, and Deep-fried Mozzarella Sandwiches, called mozzarella in carrozza. When really fresh, it can be served simply sliced on a plate with a drizzle of the very best extra virgin olive oil, to create the simplest of antipasti.

Legend has it that mozzarella was first made when cheese curds accidentally fell into a pail of hot water in a cheese factory near Naples. Mozzarella was originally made from the rich milk of water buffaloes. As it was not made from pasteurized milk and because there was little or no refrigeration, the cheese had a very short shelf life and seldom left the southern regions of Italy near Naples where it was made. As cheese technology, refrigeration and transportation systems developed, the cheese spread to other regions of Italy and is now also made using cow's milk, which is more plentiful.

Pecorino Romano, typically studded with cracked peppercorns, and fresh, soft ricotta, often made from sheep's milk or buffalo milk, are also invaluable for adding flavour to soups and antipasti.

The soups are rich and sustaining, with sturdy ingredients like rice and semolina adding bulk, an array of vegetables providing nutrients, and generous sprinklings of cheese giving a tasty finish.

The famous creation of Naples, Pizza Napoletana, the first pizza ever made, is a favourite across the world. It is delicious in its simplicity – olive oil, tomatoes, garlic, oregano and basil provide the perfect taste of classic Neapolitan cusine.

VEGETABLE SOUP WITH SEMOLINA
MINESTRA ALLA VITERBESE

This is a typical country summertime soup, prepared when all the vegetables are at their peak of luscious ripeness. This recipe is from the pretty town of Viterbo, which has quite a few age-old culinary specialities that have passed the test of time.

1 Plunge the tomato into boiling water for 30 seconds, then refresh in cold water. Remove the skin and seeds, and chop the flesh.

2 Put tomato, courgette, onion, garlic, celery, potato, carrot and herbs into a large pan. Add 1.2 litres/2 pints/5 cups cold water. Bring to the boil, cover and simmer for 15 minutes.

3 Trickle the semolina into the simmering soup in a very fine stream, stirring constantly. Simmer the soup for a further 15 minutes, stirring occasionally.

4 Remove from the heat and stir in the butter and the cheese. Allow to cool slightly before serving with extra Parmesan and butter on top.

SERVES 4

1 large, very ripe tomato
1 large courgette (zucchini), sliced into thin matchstick strips
1 large onion, sliced into rings
1 large garlic clove, finely chopped
1 large celery stick, finely chopped
1 large potato, grated
1 large carrot, grated
8 parsley sprigs, finely chopped
9 fresh basil leaves, finely chopped
50g/2oz/$^1/_3$ cup semolina
25g/1oz/2 tbsp unsalted butter, plus extra to serve
50g/2oz/$^2/_3$ cup freshly grated Parmesan cheese, plus extra to serve

PER PORTION Energy 204kcal/854kJ; Protein 8.6g; Carbohydrate 21.3g, of which sugars 6.6g; Fat 10g, of which saturates 6.1g; Cholesterol 27mg; Calcium 190mg; Fibre 2.6g; Sodium 202mg.

SERVES 4

50g/2oz/$^1/_4$ cup lard or white cooking fat
1 large onion
1kg/2$^1/_4$lb (unshelled weight) fresh broad (fava) beans, shelled and skinned (see Cook's Tip)
30ml/2 tbsp tomato purée (paste)
300ml/$^1/_2$ pint/1$^1/_4$ cups hot water
200g/7oz/1 cup short grain rice
25g/1oz unsalted butter
1 litre/1$^3/_4$ pints/4 cups boiling water
sea salt and ground black pepper
115g/4oz/1$^1/_4$ cups freshly grated Pecorino cheese, to serve

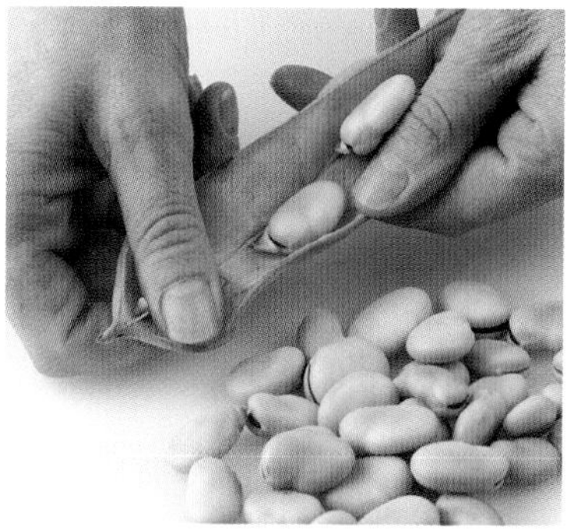

RICE AND BROAD BEAN SOUP
MINESTRA DI RISO E FAVE

From springtime onwards, broad beans are sold at roadside kiosks, which sporadically line the route from the airport into the heart of Rome. One of the most perfect flavour combinations in the world has got to be fresh, tender broad beans coupled with soft and crumbly, incredibly strong-tasting Pecorino cheese. Both reach their peak at the same time, when the ewes have plenty of milk available for their spring lambs, and extra for cheese making.

1 Chop the lard and the onion together to make a blended mass (this is called battuto in Italian). Fry this slowly in a large pan until the onion is soft. Add the beans.

2 Stir the tomato purée into the hot water and pour into the pan, then season with salt and pepper. Stir and simmer for 10 minutes.

3 Stir the rice into the soup thoroughly, then add the butter and stir again.

4 Gradually add the boiling water, stirring constantly and keeping it at a slow rolling boil.

5 Cook for about 15 minutes, until the rice is tender. Season and serve with grated Pecorino.

COOK'S TIP

To shell broad beans, split the pod down the side and push out the beans with your fingers. To skin them, place them in a bowl and pour over boiling water. Leave for 1–2 minutes then refresh in cold water. Push the beans out of their skins using your fingers.

PER PORTION Energy 507kcal/2111kJ; Protein 14.4g; Carbohydrate 61.3g, of which sugars 3.1g; Fat 22.7g, of which saturates 5.8g; Cholesterol 13mg; Calcium 87mg; Fibre 8.5g; Sodium 50mg.

SERVES 6

6 eggs
75g/3oz/1 cup freshly grated Parmesan cheese
freshly grated nutmeg or grated lemon rind, to taste
1.5 litres/2½ pints/6¼ cups rich, clear chicken stock
sea salt and ground black pepper
fresh flat leaf parsley, finely chopped, to garnish

ROMAN EGG AND CHEESE SOUP
LA STRACCIATELLA ALLA ROMANA

This light soup is much more difficult to make than it would first appear. The skill lies in making sure the delicate strands of beaten egg and cheese separate and disperse into the hot soup, rather than forming one or several large, unsightly lumps. Make the soup with a richly flavoured, clear chicken stock and ensure it is really hot, and that you pour in the egg mixture gently and with constant whisking. This is intended to be the best first course of a long Roman feast.

1 Put the eggs in a bowl and whisk until blended, then add the Parmesan cheese and season the mixture with salt and ground black pepper. Stir in the nutmeg or lemon rind.

2 About 10 minutes before you want to serve the soup, bring the stock to the boil.

3 As soon as it boils, take it off the heat. Pour in the egg mixture, whisking for 3 minutes, until the eggs have cooked enough to hold their irregularly shaped strands, floating in the broth.

4 Ladle into soup bowls and serve immediately, sprinkled with chopped parsley.

PER PORTION Energy 245kcal/1030kJ; Protein 14.1g; Carbohydrate 27.5g, of which sugars 1.3g; Fat 9.4g, of which saturates 4.1g; Cholesterol 110mg; Calcium 246mg; Fibre 1.1g; Sodium 424mg.

PANCAKES IN CHICKEN BROTH
SCRIPPELLE IN BRODO

This filling dish is deliciously warming on snowy evenings. Its success rests heavily on using a chicken stock that is really bursting with flavour. This is a classic and very typical recipe from the region of Abruzzo.

SERVES 4

4 eggs, beaten
30ml/2 tbsp milk
45ml/3 tbsp chopped fresh parsley
75g/3oz/1 cup freshly grated Parmesan cheese, plus extra to serve
1.5ml/$^1/_4$ tsp sea salt
1.5ml/$^1/_4$ tsp freshly grated nutmeg
45ml/3 tbsp plain (all-purpose) flour
1.5 litres/2$^1/_2$ pints/6$^1/_4$ cups chicken stock
30ml/2 tbsp lard or white cooking fat

1 Put the eggs and milk in a bowl, and add the parsley, 15ml/1 tbsp of the Parmesan cheese, salt and nutmeg. Beat thoroughly, then gradually beat in the flour.

2 Dilute the mixture with 30–45ml/2–3 tbsp cold water to make a batter; it should have a dropping consistency.

3 Heat the stock to boiling point and keep it simmering. Grease a 20cm/8in frying pan with lard and heat until sizzling hot.

4 Fry a small amount of the batter in the pan to make a thin pancake. Using a spatula, turn it over and cook the other side. Remove it from the pan and roll it up, then keep it warm while you make the others. Continue in this way until all the batter has been used up.

5 Arrange two or three rolled pancakes in each person's bowl and sprinkle generously with the remaining Parmesan cheese. Pour over the stock to cover, and serve immediately, with extra Parmesan, if you like.

PER PORTION Energy 270kcal/1123kJ; Protein 15.1g; Carbohydrate 9.3g, of which sugars 0.6g; Fat 19.6g, of which saturates 8.6g; Cholesterol 216mg; Calcium 280mg; Fibre 0.4g; Sodium 483mg.

DEEP-FRIED MOZZARELLA SANDWICHES
MOZZARELLA IN CARROZZA

The word carrozza means carriage, and these deep-fried sandwiches are the perfect vessel to carry luxurious mozzarella. It is quite a heavy dish, so when served as an antipasto it should be followed by a light main course.

1 Trim the bread to slightly larger than the mozzarella slices. Lay four slices of bread on a board and spread each one with anchovy paste. Cover the anchovy paste with two slices of mozzarella. Season with black pepper, and cover with the other slices of bread. Squash these sandwiches together very firmly.

2 Put the beaten eggs into a shallow bowl. Slide the sandwiches into the eggs and leave to soak for 15 minutes.

3 Meanwhile, pour enough sunflower oil into a wide, deep frying pan to a depth of about 7.5cm/3in. Heat until a small cube of bread, dropped into the oil, sizzles instantly.

4 Fry the four sandwiches in the hot oil until crisp and golden on both sides, remove with a metal spatula and drain thoroughly on kitchen paper. Serve piping hot, with tomato salad or a bowl of tomato sauce offered separately, if you like.

SERVES 4

8 slices white bread, crusts removed
7.5ml/1½ tsp anchovy paste
250g/9oz mozzarella, cut into 8 thick slices
3 eggs, beaten
sunflower oil, for deep-frying
ground black pepper
tomato salad or tomato sauce (see page 21), to serve (optional)

PER PORTION Energy 428kcal/1789kJ; Protein 18.9g; Carbohydrate 30.5g, of which sugars 2.7g; Fat 26.6g, of which saturates 10.4g; Cholesterol 129mg; Calcium 331mg; Fibre 1.9g; Sodium 539mg.

SERVES 4

300g/11oz provatura or scamorza cheese
1 small loaf of crusty bread or sliced white bread
150g/5oz/10 tbsp unsalted butter
2 large salted anchovies, boned, rinsed and patted dry on kitchen paper
30ml/2 tbsp milk
ground black pepper

CHEESE SKEWERS WITH ANCHOVY SAUCE
SPIEDINI DI PROVATURA

Provatura is basically a Roman version of mozzarella. It tends to be slightly more solid and less creamy than mozzarella. If you can't get hold of it, use scamorza (matured and sometimes smoked mozzarella) or fresh mozzarella that has been allowed to harden slightly over three or four days. In fact, this is a useful recipe for using up mozzarella that is past its best. It's perfect cooked over a barbecue, but can be cooked under a grill too. You could offer the anchovy sauce separately, if you prefer.

1 Soak four wooden skewers in water for 30 minutes. Cut the cheese and bread into equal-sized pieces about 2cm/¾in thick.

2 Thread the cheese and bread alternately on to the skewers, making sure that they are packed together as tightly as possible.

3 Cook the skewers on a barbecue or under a grill (broiler) until the cheese is just running and the bread is crisp.

4 Meanwhile, put the butter and anchovies into a small pan and warm over a low heat (you can do this on a corner of the barbecue), stirring constantly until the anchovies have been reduced to a smooth cream.

5 Stir in the milk as the mixture begins to amalgamate. Season with black pepper.

6 Arrange the skewers on a serving platter, cover with the anchovy sauce and serve hot.

PER PORTION Energy 712kcal/2971kJ; Protein 23.2g; Carbohydrate 49.7g, of which sugars 3g; Fat 48.2g, of which saturates 31g; Cholesterol 130mg; Calcium 401mg; Fibre 1.5g; Sodium 1161mg.

SERVES 4

115g/4oz/1 cup finely cubed Gruyère cheese
75g/3oz/$^3/_4$ cup chopped prosciutto crudo
25ml/1$^1/_2$ tbsp freshly grated Parmesan cheese
1 egg, beaten
300g/11oz/2$^2/_3$ cups plain (all-purpose) flour
50g/2oz/$^1/_4$ cup unsalted butter, cubed
2 egg yolks
1 egg white, lightly beaten until frothy
sunflower oil, for deep-frying
sea salt and ground black pepper

ROMAN CHEESE AND HAM FRITTERS
PANZEROTTI ALLA ROMANA

Probably one of the earliest recipes from the culinary history of the great city of Rome, these rich and savoury dough fritters would traditionally be served as an antipasto or a snack; at some time in their history they were probably cooked as street food and sold from sizzling cauldrons of boiling oil to hungry passers-by. You can vary the contents of the filling according to personal taste; for example, mozzarella or scamorza can be used instead of the Gruyère, and salami or cooked ham could be used instead of the prosciutto crudo.

1 Mix the cubed cheese with the prosciutto, Parmesan cheese and the beaten whole egg. Season with a little salt and ground black pepper, and set aside until required.

2 Put the flour in a mound on the work surface. Plunge your fist into the centre to make a hollow. Put a pinch of salt, the butter and the egg yolks into the hollow. Blend together with your fingertips, adding 30–45ml/2–3 tbsp cold water, if necessary.

3 When you have achieved a smooth ball of dough, roll it out as thinly as possible.

4 Use a 5cm/2in pastry (cookie) cutter or inverted tumbler to cut out circles of dough.

5 Put a spoonful of the cheese mixture on to each circle and fold in half. Brush the edges with a little beaten egg white, and seal the panzerotti closed.

6 Heat the oil for deep-frying in a deep pan until a small piece of the pastry, dropped into the oil, sizzles instantly. Fry the panzerotti for 5 minutes, or until golden brown and puffy.

7 Drain on kitchen paper and serve hot.

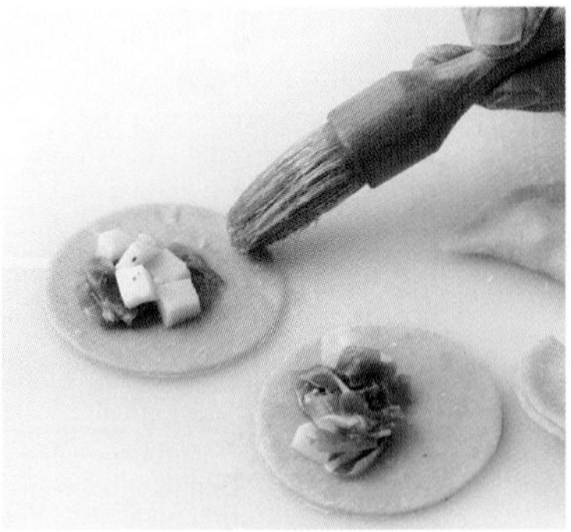

PER PORTION Energy 436kcal/1800kJ; Protein 17g; Carbohydrate 0.2g, of which sugars 0.2g; Fat 40.2g, of which saturates 17.3g; Cholesterol 222mg; Calcium 310mg; Fibre 0g; Sodium 632mg.

POTATO CROQUETTES
CROCCHÈ DI PATATE

These crisp little potato patties are hugely popular in Naples as a snack or as part of an antipasto course. They are a legacy of the French chefs who, in the late 1800s and early 1900s, were employed to cook in the large houses of the grand aristocracy; the wealthy southern Italian families believed that the presence of a French chef raised their profile. In the same way that the word croquette was corrupted to a much more Italian-sounding crocchè, the name for the household French chef became Monsu, as opposed to Monsieur.

SERVES 6

1kg/2¹/₄lb unpeeled floury potatoes, scrubbed
65g/2¹/₂oz/3 tbsp unsalted butter, melted
60ml/4 tbsp freshly grated Parmesan cheese
30ml/2 tbsp finely chopped fresh parsley
2 eggs, separated
75g/3oz/²/₃ cup plain (all-purpose) flour, for coating
75g/3oz/generous 1 cup fine dried breadcrumbs
1 litre/1³/₄ pints/4 cups sunflower oil, for deep-frying
sea salt and ground black pepper

1 Put the potatoes in a large pan, cover with cold water and boil until softened. Drain and peel while they are hot, and then push them through a food mill with large holes several times. If you do not have a food mill, mash them thoroughly or push them through a ricer. Mix and blend the potatoes until smooth.

2 Add the butter, Parmesan and parsley, then season with salt and pepper. Gradually blend in the egg yolks, one at a time.

3 Work the mixture with your hands until thoroughly mixed, then shape it into croquettes.

4 Put the flour on a plate. Put the egg whites in a bowl, and whisk until foaming. Put the breadcrumbs on another plate. Dip each croquette in the flour until coated all over, then dip it into the egg whites, and finally coat in the breadcrumbs.

5 Heat the oil in a large pan to 180°C/350°F, or until a small cube of bread browns in 40 seconds.

6 Fry the croquettes until crisp and golden, then drain on kitchen paper and serve them piping hot.

PER PORTION Energy 502kcal/2095kJ; Protein 11.5g; Carbohydrate 46.2g, of which sugars 2.7g; Fat 31.4g, of which saturates 10.6g; Cholesterol 98mg; Calcium 175mg; Fibre 2.3g; Sodium 327mg.

CALZONE WITH TOMATO SAUCE
CALZONE CON SALSA DI POMODORO

The word calzone means 'stocking' or 'trouser' in Italian (with the plural calzoni translating as 'trousers'), as it is supposed to look like a folded pair of pantaloons! Here the calzoni are filled with tomato, ricotta cheese and salami, but you can vary the filling according to your personal taste or the season – try experimenting with whatever ingredients you have in your refrigerator. This recipe is from the bustling city of Naples and is now a world-wide classic, featuring on many Italian restaurant menus.

1 To make the tomato sauce, heat the olive oil in a pan over a low heat and fry the garlic for 5 minutes without browning. Add the tomatoes and stir together.

2 Bring to the tomato sauce to the boil and simmer for 15 minutes. Add salt and pepper to taste, then stir in the chopped parsley.

3 Preheat the oven to 200°C/400°C/Gas 6. Oil a baking sheet and sprinkle it lightly with semolina.

4 Cut the pizza dough into four equal pieces, then roll each into a circle about 20cm/8in in diameter.

5 Spread the ricotta cheese over one half of each circle of dough, keeping the edges clear so that you can fold it in half and seal it.

6 Sprinkle the salami, sun-dried tomatoes and parsley on top of the ricotta cheese. Drizzle with a little olive oil and season lightly with salt and pepper.

7 Using a metal spatula, lift each calzone on to the baking sheet. Fold each calzone in half and seal the open edge firmly with the back of a fork.

8 Bake in the preheated oven for 15 minutes, or until they are golden, then serve with the tomato sauce offered separately.

SERVES 4

extra virgin olive oil, for greasing and drizzling
semolina, for dusting
1 quantity Basic Pizza Dough (see page 19)
30ml/2 tbsp fresh ricotta cheese
3 slices salami, coarsely chopped
2 sun-dried tomatoes in olive oil, drained and chopped
15ml/1 tbsp chopped fresh flat leaf parsley
sea salt and ground black pepper

FOR THE SAUCE

30ml/2 tbsp extra virgin olive oil
2 garlic cloves, finely chopped
400g/14oz can chopped tomatoes
30ml/2 tbsp chopped fresh flat leaf parsley

VARIATIONS

- You can also make two large calzoni. They will take 20–25 minutes to bake.
- Or you can make eight mini calzoni: divide the dough into eight equal pieces, fill and seal, then deep-fry them in sunflower oil until golden.

PER PORTION Energy 732kcal/3071kJ; Protein 20g; Carbohydrate 97.4g, of which sugars 9.7g; Fat 31.9g, of which saturates 8.7g; Cholesterol 22mg; Calcium 329mg; Fibre 7.8g; Sodium 1142mg.

MAKES 6 SINGLE PIZZAS

1 quantity Basic Pizza Dough (see page 19)
30ml/2 tbsp passata (bottled strained tomatoes) or chopped fresh tomatoes
4 garlic cloves, finely chopped
7.5ml/1½ tsp dried oregano
60ml/4 tbsp olive oil, plus extra for greasing
18 fresh basil leaves
sea salt and ground black pepper
green salad, to serve (optional)

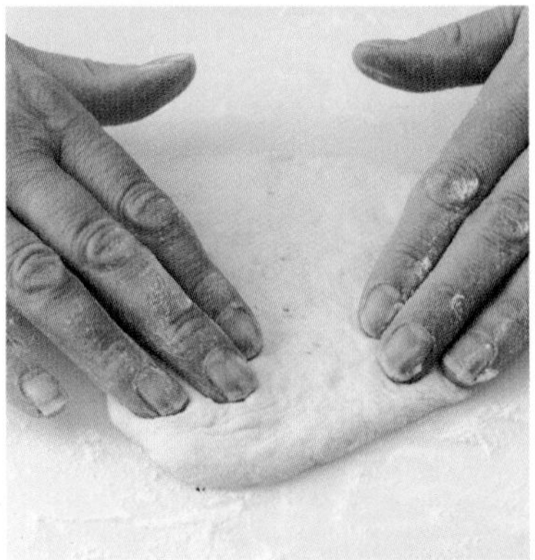

PIZZA NAPOLETANA
LA PIZZA NAPOLETANA

Although pizzas can be topped with all kinds of savouries, the Napoletana is the much-loved classic recipe for the first pizza ever created, and it is named after the city where it is believed to have first been made: Naples. It is interesting that although the original recipe, and the concept of this Italian speciality, have become a global phenomenon over the years, the name of the baker or cook who first created it has seemingly been forgotten.

1 Preheat the oven to 220°C/425°F/Gas 7 and lightly oil two baking sheets. Divide the dough into six equal pieces. Roll or press out each piece thinly and transfer to the baking sheets.

2 Cover thinly with the passata or chopped tomatoes, leaving a border of about 2.5cm/1in around the edges.

3 Sprinkle each pizza with the garlic, oregano, olive oil, basil and a little salt and ground black pepper.

4 Bake for 5–10 minutes until the border is crisp and well cooked and the pizzas are dry underneath (lift up one edge to check). Serve immediately, with salad leaves, if you like.

PER PORTION Energy 488kcal/2059kJ; Protein 12g; Carbohydrate 82.7g, of which sugars 10.4g; Fat 14.4g, of which saturates 1.2g; Cholesterol 0mg; Calcium 145mg; Fibre 5.1g; Sodium 382mg.

MOLISAN BREAD AND TOMATO SALAD
ACQUA SALE

The simple, but delicious, fresh tomato salad from the tiny region of Molise has a soft bread base, making it similar in principle to the Tuscan salad panzanella. Don't skimp on the dried oregano – the one herb that is always much more delicious when used dried instead of fresh – as this will bring the salad vibrantly to life. Lots of good-quality olive oil is used to give the salad extra richness. Choose the sweetest and ripest tomatoes you can find, while they are in season.

SERVES 6

- 2.5ml/½ tsp sea salt
- 4 thick slices of crusty, rustic bread, such as casareccio
- 4 large, ripe tomatoes, chopped
- 1 garlic clove, finely chopped
- 10ml/2 tsp dried oregano
- 300ml/½ pint/1¼ cups extra virgin olive oil

1 Dissolve the salt in 500ml/17fl oz/generous 2 cups water. Dampen the slices of bread with the salted water and lay them out on a platter.

2 Arrange the chopped tomatoes on top.

3 Sprinkle with the chopped garlic and the dried oregano.

4 Drizzle with the olive oil and leave to stand for an hour before serving.

PER PORTION Energy 395kcal/1636kJ; Protein 3.7g; Carbohydrate 19.1g, of which sugars 3.2g; Fat 34.3g, of which saturates 4.7g; Cholesterol 0mg; Calcium 58mg; Fibre 1.6g; Sodium 186mg.

TOMATO, MOZZARELLA AND BASIL SALAD
LA CAPRESE

This classic summer salad of tomatoes and mozzarella comes from the beautiful island of Capri. The juice from the tomatoes and the whey from the cheese will seep out to create liquid around the salad – this is delicious soaked up with plenty of crusty bread. The cheese should be perfectly fresh and juicy, whether it is made from buffalo milk or not. The basil leaves must always be torn, and never cut with a knife or scissors, because this alters the flavour and blackens the leaves.

1 Slice the tomatoes and the mozzarella into even slices, cubes or chunks.

2 Put them into a salad bowl and mix them together with your hands.

3 Sprinkle with the oil and mix together again with a spoon. Add the basil.

4 Season to taste, and mix again. Leave to stand for 15 minutes before serving.

SERVES 4

2 very large, firm tomatoes (about the same size as the mozzarella balls)
2 x 125g mozzarella balls, drained
90ml/6 tbsp extra virgin olive oil
about 24 fresh basil leaves, torn into small pieces
sea salt and ground black pepper

COOK'S TIP

Be careful not to add too much salt to the salad, as some mozzarella may already be quite salty.

PER PORTION Energy 326kcal/1350kJ; Protein 12.3g; Carbohydrate 3.1g, of which sugars 3.1g; Fat 29.5g, of which saturates 11g; Cholesterol 36mg; Calcium 233mg; Fibre 1g; Sodium 256mg.

SERVES 4

4 large oranges
8 small anchovy fillets, canned in olive oil, drained
45ml/3 tbsp extra virgin olive oil
sea salt and ground black pepper

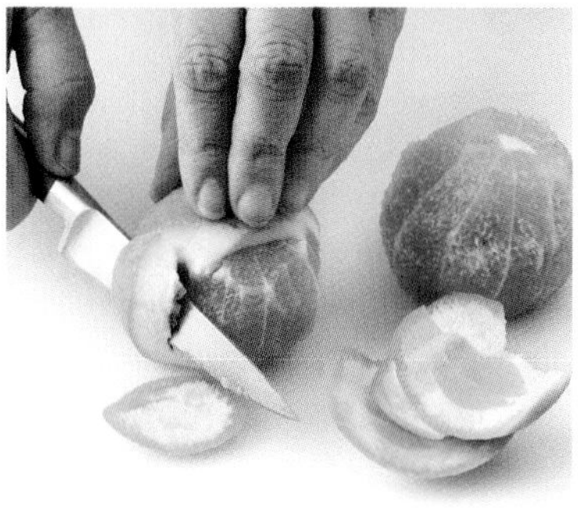

PER PORTION Energy 147kcal/612kJ; Protein 3.2g; Carbohydrate 12.8g, of which sugars 12.8g; Fat 9.6g, of which saturates 1.2g; Cholesterol 0mg; Calcium 89mg; Fibre 2.6g; Sodium 243mg.

ORANGE ANTIPASTO
ANTIPASTO DI ARANCE

Anchovies go surprisingly well with orange in this very simple salad from the Abruzzo region. The fresh and zingy citrus flavour, enhanced by the salty anchovies, is guaranteed to sharpen the tastebuds.

1 Place each orange on a plate and cut off the peel and pith in strips using a sharp knife. Cut the remaining peel and pith from each end of the oranges.

2 Slice the orange and arrange on a platter.

3 Arrange the anchovy fillets on top of the slices of orange.

4 Drizzle with the extra virgin olive oil. Season with salt and ground black pepper, and serve.

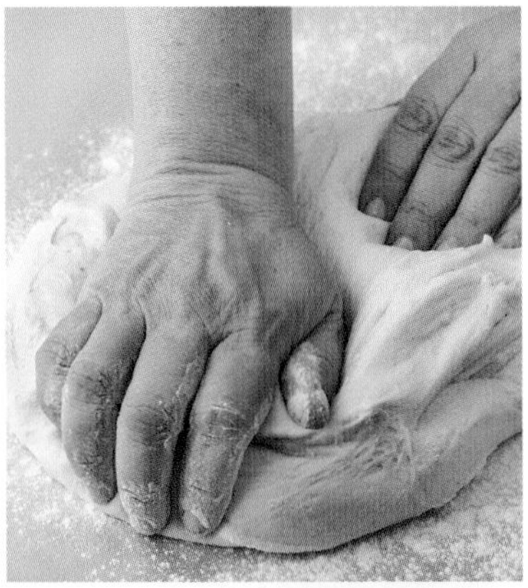

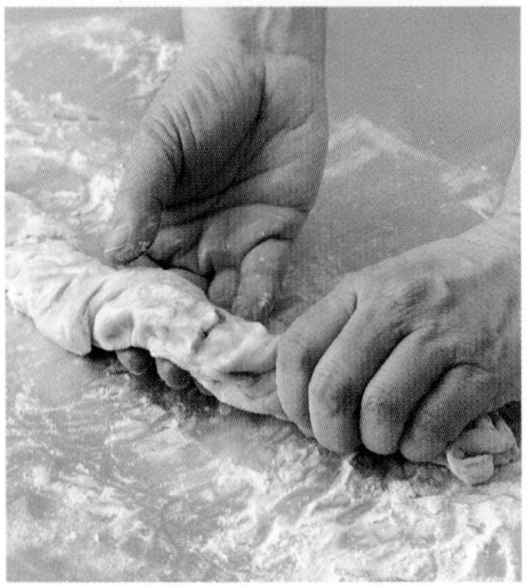

SARDINIAN FOCACCIA TWIST
'NFIGGHIULATA

This lovely sticky loaf made with ricotta and salami is delicious eaten simply on its own (perhaps with a glass of local wine), but it is especially good when served as part of an antipasto selection with olives, cured meats and strong-flavoured Sardinian Pecorino cheese. It has a bit of a kick as it contains a good pinch of dried chilli flakes, but you can, of course, vary the heat by increasing or decreasing the amount of chilli added according to your own taste.

SERVES 6

450g/1lb/4 cups strong white bread flour
30g/1$^{1}/_{4}$oz fresh yeast
about 300ml/$^{1}/_{2}$ pint/1$^{1}/_{4}$ cups warm water
pinch of sugar
sea salt
90–120ml/6–8 tbsp extra virgin olive oil, plus extra for greasing
350g/12oz fresh ricotta cheese, drained overnight in a colander
300g/11oz salami, chopped
large pinch coarsely ground dried chilli flakes

1 Put the flour on to the work surface and make a hollow in the centre. In a small bowl, mix the yeast and warm water together. Mix in the sugar and about 30ml/2 tbsp of the flour.

2 Put the yeast mixture in a warm place to activate for 30 minutes, or until the froth begins to appear on the surface.

3 When the yeast mixture is fizzing gently, add it to the hollow in the flour. Combine it together, then knead it energetically into the remaining flour, adding a little more water if necessary.

4 Add the salt and the oil, and knead the dough well for about 10 minutes until soft, elastic and slightly shiny. Transfer the dough to a large, floured bowl.

5 Oil the underside of a piece of clear film (plastic wrap) to prevent it sticking against the rising dough, and use it to cover the bowl. Put the bowl in a warm place and leave it to rise for about 2 hours, or until doubled in size.

6 Preheat the oven to 220°C/425°F/Gas 7 and oil a baking sheet. Roll out the risen dough thinly and brush the surface generously with oil.

7 Cover half the dough with the ricotta and salami, and add a sprinkling of chilli.

8 Fold the dough in half to cover the filling, then roll the focaccia up on itself, brushing the dough's surface generously with oil on each turn.

9 Transfer the focaccia to the baking sheet and bake in the preheated oven for 30–35 minutes, or until it is lightly golden.

10 Remove the focaccia from the oven, cover loosely with foil and leave to cool.

11 Serve, sliced, either at room temperature or while still slightly warm.

VARIATION

If you like, you could add chopped garlic, sliced raw onion or chopped fresh tomatoes to the basic filling, with or without the salami.

PER PORTION Energy 705kcal/2943kJ; Protein 22.1g; Carbohydrate 61g, of which sugars 2.9g; Fat 43g, of which saturates 7g; Cholesterol 64mg; Calcium 110mg; Fibre 2.4g; Sodium 927mg.

PASTA, GNOCCHI AND RICE

PASTA, GNOCCHI E RISO

Lazio, Campania, Abruzzo and Molise share a passion for dried pasta, and each region has its traditional shapes. Sardinia also has its own pasta culture, but it is quite individual, reflecting the kaleidoscope of variations within Italy's cuisines. Sardinia favours the small, toasted fregola, which is similar to large-grained couscous, or the little shell-shaped pasta, malloreddus. In Lazio, the strong flavours in the local dishes are matched by the chunky shapes of bucatini or rigatoni. In Campania, spaghetti rules supreme. The people of Abruzzo are rightfully proud of their handmade, square spaghetti. It is known as spaghetti alla chitarra, because the tool used to make it is like a guitar with tight strings, which cuts the pasta neatly under the pressure of a rolling pin. Durum wheat has always grown profusely in Molise and this region produces some of the best flour for pasta making.

DURUM WHEAT PASTA AND FLAVOURSOME SAUCES

Some of the most well-known pasta dishes come from the regions of Lazio and Campania, such as the strident Puttanesca Pasta, the ingeniously simple Spaghetti with Oil and Garlic, or the delectable Pasta Carbonara. Lesser known, but no less delicious, are the pasta specialities of Abruzzo, Molise and Sardinia. Sardinia's famous bottarga, or dried fish roe, can be delicately shaved, like a truffle, all over freshly cooked pasta and then gently moistened with just a drizzle of the very best extra virgin olive oil. Dried durum wheat pasta takes precedence in this area of Italy, and Rome's pasta dishes are legendary. They are often so rich and filling they can constitute an entire meal (rather than being served as a primo), and can be abundantly flavoured with anchovies, capers, garlic, chilli and pancetta. Most important of all in these pasta dishes is the tomato. World-famous tomato sauce, in all its variations, remains one of the most perfect accompaniments for pasta that has ever been created.

A wonderful version of gnocchi belongs exclusively to Rome, gnocchi alla Romana, or Roman Semolina Gnocchi. It is made from semolina boiled in milk, thickened with egg yolks and enriched with Parmesan. The resulting dish is substantial, but delicate in flavour.

Risotto is quite rare in these regions, although Sardinia, with its historical link to Piedmont and some locally grown rice, does feature a few examples of this famous rice dish. The intense flavour of saffron features in the unusal Sardinian Saffron Risotto, which also contains pork and tomatoes, making it very different to the risottos of the Veneto. A tasty Squid Risotto from Lazio is featured in this chapter too, which contains the bold flavours we expect from this region.

PASTA WITH TOMATOES AND MOZZARELLA
PASTA ALLA CAPRESE

Ripe tomatoes and mozzarella, with the pungent flavouring of oregano, are used in this delicious dish from the beautiful island of Capri. One thing to note is that pasta in Campania is served extremely al dente, which can be a bit of a shock for tourists!

1 Bring a large pan of lightly salted water to a rolling boil. Put the pasta into the water and stir. Return to the boil and cook for 8 minutes, or according to pack instructions, until al dente. Reserve the pasta cooking water.

2 Meanwhile, mix the tomatoes and mozzarella in a large bowl.

3 Add the olive oil and oregano to the tomatoes and mozzarella. Season with salt and pepper, then tear the basil leaves and add to the bowl.

4 When the pasta is ready, add it to the bowl with approximately 120ml/4fl oz/½ cup of the pasta water. Mix well and serve immediately.

SERVES 4

450g/1lb fusilli lunghi or spaghetti
2 large tomatoes, diced
2 x 125g/4½oz mozzarella balls, cubed
60ml/4 tbsp extra virgin olive oil
5ml/1 tsp dried oregano
4 fresh basil leaves
sea salt and ground black pepper

COOK'S TIP

Use a good quality extra virgin olive oil to achieve the most authentic flavour for this dish.

PER PORTION Energy 657kcal/2766kJ; Protein 25.7g; Carbohydrate 85.7g, of which sugars 6g; Fat 25.9g, of which saturates 10.4g; Cholesterol 36mg; Calcium 260mg; Fibre 4g; Sodium 257mg.

SERVES 4

400g/14oz spaghetti or spaghettini
175ml/6fl oz/$^{3}/_{4}$ cup extra virgin olive oil
3 garlic cloves, crushed
30ml/2 tbsp chopped fresh flat leaf parsley
sea salt and ground black pepper

SPAGHETTI WITH OIL AND GARLIC
SPAGHETTI AJO E OJO

Lots of versions of this classic Roman recipe exist, but this is a traditional one. It is reputedly very good for preventing a hangover when consumed last thing at night. Another version, Ajo Ojo e Peperoncino, includes chilli, making it quite fiery.

1 Bring a large pan of lightly salted water to a rolling boil. Add the pasta and stir. Return to the boil and cook the pasta according to the pack instructions until al dente.

2 Meanwhile, heat the oil and garlic together until the garlic turns black. Discard the garlic and keep the oil hot. Timing is crucial, as the oil must not burn; although it must be hot.

3 Drain the cooked pasta and return it to the hot pan. Pour over the flavoured oil and mix together to thoroughly coat the pasta in the oil.

4 Season the pasta with plenty of ground black pepper and mix in the chopped parsley. Transfer to a warmed serving platter and serve immediately.

PER PORTION Energy 505kcal/2126kJ; Protein 12.8g; Carbohydrate 76.4g, of which sugars 3.5g; Fat 18.6g, of which saturates 2.6g; Cholesterol 0mg; Calcium 27mg; Fibre 3.3g; Sodium 3mg.

SERVES 6

45ml/3 tbsp extra virgin olive oil
3 garlic cloves, chopped
900g/2lb canned Italian plum tomatoes, chopped and juice reserved
450g/1lb rigatoni
250g/9oz ricotta cheese
30ml/2 tbsp torn fresh basil
45ml/3 tbsp freshly grated Parmesan cheese
sea salt and ground black pepper

RIGATONI WITH TOMATO AND RICOTTA
RIGATONI AL POMODORO E RICOTTA

With its broad shape and fine ridges, rigatoni is the most perfect pasta to suit this particular sauce of clingy ricotta cheese and tomato. It is a superbly simple dish, but very filling and satisfying – a real family favourite for many Italians.

1 Pour the oil into a medium pan. Add the garlic and heat for about 3 minutes, or until it is just translucent.

2 Add the tomatoes and their juice, and simmer over a low heat for 50 minutes, or until the liquid has evaporated.

3 Bring a large pan of lightly salted water to a rolling boil. Add the pasta and stir. Return to the boil and cook according to the pack instructions until al dente.

4 Meanwhile, put the ricotta cheese into a heatproof bowl and crumble it with a fork. Set the bowl in a pan of hot water and leave to heat the cheese.

5 Add the basil to the tomato sauce and season with salt and pepper. Stir. Drain the pasta and transfer it to a warm serving bowl.

6 Add the tomato sauce and half the ricotta cheese. Toss gently. Cover with the remaining ricotta, sprinkle with Parmesan, and serve.

PER PORTION Energy 443kcal/1867kJ; Protein 17.1g; Carbohydrate 61.7g, of which sugars 8.6g; Fat 15.9g, of which saturates 6.4g; Cholesterol 25mg; Calcium 136mg; Fibre 4.1g; Sodium 100mg.

MACCHERONI WITH SEVEN FLAVOURS
MACCHERONI AI SETTE ODORI

This is the most famous dish from the lovely village of Positano. Few things are more inspiring and beautiful than the views from the top of the cliff there, or the incredible winding road that takes you out of the chaos of Naples into the bright sunlight and greenery of the coastline. The sauce for this dish is best made the day before, although you can also make it about 3 hours in advance. Ripe, soft and fresh tomatoes are essential to accompany the seven flavours of garlic, olive oil, basil, parsley, oregano, onion and celery. In Campania, maccheroni is often a generic term for pasta, so you can use any other pasta shape for this dish. As the sauce is served cold, the dish will be lukewarm.

SERVES 4

600g/1lb 5oz ripe tomatoes
1 garlic clove, crushed
45ml/3 tbsp olive oil
10 fresh basil leaves, torn into small shreds
30ml/2 tbsp chopped fresh parsley
5ml/1 tsp dried oregano
½ onion, very finely chopped
1 celery stick, very finely chopped
400g/14oz maccheroni
salt and ground black pepper

1 Plunge the tomatoes into boiling water for 30 seconds, then refresh in cold water. Peel away the skins. Cut them in half and remove the seeds. Quarter and place in a colander, set over a bowl, to drain for 30 minutes.

2 When the tomatoes are drained, discard their juice and transfer them to a bowl. Add the garlic, olive oil, basil, parsley, oregano, onion and celery, and stir carefully into the tomatoes.

3 Season with salt and pepper, and leave to stand overnight or for at least 2 hours.

4 When you are ready to serve, bring a large pan of lightly salted water to a rolling boil. Add the maccheroni and stir. Return to the boil and cook for 8 minutes or according to the pack instructions until al dente.

5 Drain and return to the pan. Pour over the sauce and stir together. Serve immediately.

PER PORTION Energy 456kcal/1928kJ; Protein 13.8g; Carbohydrate 81.1g, of which sugars 9.7g; Fat 10.7g, of which saturates 1.5g; Cholesterol 0mg; Calcium 70mg; Fibre 5.5g; Sodium 26mg.

PASTA CARBONARA
PASTA ALLA CARBONARA

This classic dish has two very different stories relating to its origins. The first tells us of the carbonari, or charcoal burners, living on the banks of rivers like the Tiber. These families lived with just a few basics: a sheep for milk and cheese, a few hens for eggs, and a pig for fresh and cured meats. Their lives were dusted with a scattering of black charcoal flakes and the ever-present soft smoke. So the recipe honours these people, by putting together the cheese, eggs and pancetta, and the ground black pepper represents the flakes of charcoal. Some think it was a more recent invention, created to feed the American GIs at the end of the Second World War because they constantly demanded 'ham and eggs', and the locals obliged with this creation!

SERVES 4

400g/14oz bucatini or spaghetti
200g/7oz pancetta, guanciale or best-quality streaky (fatty) bacon, cubed
3 eggs, beaten
75ml/5 tbsp freshly grated Pecorino or Parmesan cheese, plus extra to serve
sea salt and ground black pepper

1 Bring a large pan of lightly salted water to a rolling boil. Add the pasta and stir. Return to the boil and cook according to the pack instructions until al dente.

2 While the pasta is cooking, dry-fry the pancetta, guanciale or bacon in a very hot frying pan until crisp and the fat has run freely.

3 Beat the eggs in a bowl with the cheese and plenty of freshly ground black pepper.

4 When the pasta is cooked, drain it and return it to the pan, then turn off the heat.

5 Immediately pour the egg mixture and the pancetta into the pan, and stir everything together so that the eggs scramble very lightly and bring the other ingredients together. The fat from the pancetta should sizzle as it mingles with the pasta.

6 Serve sprinkled with cheese and black pepper.

PER PORTION Energy 620kcal/2609kJ; Protein 32g; Carbohydrate 74.1g, of which sugars 3.3g; Fat 23.9g, of which saturates 9.3g; Cholesterol 194mg; Calcium 275mg; Fibre 2.9g; Sodium 890mg.

SERVES 4

45ml/3 tbsp extra virgin olive oil
300g/11oz pancetta, cubed
1 onion, finely chopped
3 garlic cloves, chopped
½–2 dried red chillies, seeded and finely chopped
400g/14oz can chopped tomatoes
400g/14oz bucatini or other chunky dried durum wheat pasta
75g/3oz/1 cup freshly grated Pecorino or Parmesan cheese
sea salt and ground black pepper

PER PORTION Energy 725kcal/3043kJ; Protein 31.9g; Carbohydrate 77.2g, of which sugars 6.4g; Fat 34.2g, of which saturates 11.5g; Cholesterol 68mg; Calcium 262mg; Fibre 3.9g; Sodium 1162mg.

BUCATINI WITH AMATRICIANA SAUCE
BUCATINI ALL'AMATRICIANA

From the little town of Amatrice, in Lazio, comes this classic sauce. It has many fans, and is one of those recipes that cause a great deal of argument and discussion among aficionados: Should the bacon be pancetta or guanciale? Is it right to use both onion and garlic? Should it not be one or the other? How much chilli, and what kind of chilli, makes this sauce just right? There are no clear answers to these questions, and the sauce remains one of those that can be tinkered with until it is exactly as you like it.

1 Heat the oil in a pan and fry the cubed pancetta until the fat is transparent and running freely.

2 Add the onion, garlic and chillies to the pan and fry together gently until the onion is translucent and soft. Add the tomatoes.

3 Cover and simmer for 20 minutes, stirring frequently until the sauce is thick and glossy.

4 Bring a large pan of lightly salted water to a rolling boil. Add the pasta and stir. Return to the boil and cook the pasta according to the pack instructions until al dente.

5 Drain the pasta thoroughly and return to the pan, then pour in the sauce and mix together.

6 Serve sprinkled with the cheese and a little black pepper.

SERVES 4

150ml/¼ pint/⅔ cup olive oil
1 large onion, very thinly sliced
3 thick slices prosciutto crudo, cubed
1 garlic clove, chopped
1 hot dried red chilli
400g/14oz tagliolini
15ml/1 tbsp chopped fresh parsley
sea salt

TAGLIOLINI WITH HAM, ONION AND CHILLI
TAGLIOLINI ALLA MOLISANA

The ancient tradition of excellence in pasta making has made the region of Molise famous all over the world. Although the good old-fashioned, hand-made pasta is still lovingly prepared in many households, Molise also makes top-quality industrially prepared pasta, with brands such as La Molisana and Guacci showing off their expertise. You can choose from the huge variety of local factory-made durum wheat pasta available: zite, zitoni, canneroncini, conchiglie and many other shapes.

1 Heat the oil gently in a large, wide frying pan. Add the onion, prosciutto, garlic and dried chilli. Mix together and simmer slowly for 40 minutes.

2 Bring a large pan of lightly salted water to a rolling boil. Add the pasta and stir.

3 Return to the boil and cook according to the pack instructions until al dente. Drain. Transfer to the frying pan with the onion mixture.

4 Stir everything together over the heat for 2 minutes, sprinkle with the parsley and serve immediately.

PER PORTION Energy 616kcal/2588kJ; Protein 16.7g; Carbohydrate 80.3g, of which sugars 7.8g; Fat 27.6g, of which saturates 3.9g; Cholesterol 11mg; Calcium 49mg; Fibre 4g; Sodium 231mg.

PUTTANESCA PASTA
LA PUTTANESCA

This sauce is named after the famous Roman 'ladies of the night', who are as strident, garish and obvious as the bold flavours of this sauce. The key here is that all the ingredients should sing out so that you can taste each one individually, as well as blending beautifully to create the overall taste of the sauce. It is crucial not to add the olives until the end of cooking, and not to omit the dried oregano, which is absolutely essential for the flavour.

SERVES 4

120ml/4fl oz/$^1/_2$ cup extra virgin olive oil
1–3 garlic cloves, peeled and lightly crushed
3 anchovy fillets (either salted or canned in oil), rinsed and patted dry on kitchen paper
1–3 small dried red chillies, according to taste, finely chopped
25ml/1$^1/_2$ tbsp salted capers, rinsed, dried and chopped
300g/11oz passata (bottled strained tomatoes) or canned chopped tomatoes
5ml/1 tsp dried oregano
90ml/6 tbsp dry white wine
400g/14oz penne or spaghetti
a handful of pitted black olives
30ml/2 tbsp chopped fresh flat leaf parsley
sea salt and ground black pepper

1 Heat half the oil in a pan and fry the garlic with the anchovy fillets and dried chillies, until the anchovies disintegrate.

2 Add the capers and passata or tomatoes, and stir together thoroughly. Simmer for 5 minutes, then add the oregano, salt and pepper, and wine. Stir, then simmer gently for at least 15 minutes, or up to 30 minutes if you have time.

3 Meanwhile, bring a large pan of lightly salted water to a rolling boil. Add the pasta and stir. Return to the boil and cook according to the pack instructions until al dente. Drain and return to the pan.

4 Add the olives to the sauce and stir through. Pour the sauce over the pasta and add the remaining olive oil and the parsley. Toss together and serve.

PER PORTION Energy 592kcal/2489kJ; Protein 14.5g; Carbohydrate 77g, of which sugars 6.1g; Fat 25.8g, of which saturates 3.5g; Cholesterol 0mg; Calcium 88mg; Fibre 5g; Sodium 726mg.

SPAGHETTI WITH CLAMS
SPAGHETTI ALLE VONGOLE

This is an absolute classic of southern Italian cooking, and depends on the careful preparation of really fresh clams for the best result. As with all recipes using clams, do make sure that they are as clean as possible before you cook them to avoid an unpleasant muddy taste or a gritty sensation between your teeth. Rinse them in several changes of water until the water runs clear. Many different versions of this traditional dish exist all over the country, but this one is from Campania.

SERVES 4

1.5kg/3¼lb fresh baby clams
90ml/6 tbsp extra virgin olive oil
3 garlic cloves, finely chopped
400g/14oz spaghetti or vermicelli
45ml/3 tbsp chopped fresh flat leaf parsley
sea salt and ground black pepper

1 Scrub the clams thoroughly in several changes of fresh water to make sure you have removed all traces of sand or mud. When the water is completely clear, the clams are clean. Discard any clams that do not close when sharply tapped on a work surface.

2 Drain the clams and put them into a wide, fairly deep frying pan with 30ml/2 tbsp of the oil. Cover the pan and put it over a high heat.

3 When the pan is hot, shake it regularly over the heat for 6–7 minutes, to open the clams up. Discard any clams that remain closed after this time.

4 Meanwhile bring a large pan of salted water to the boil for the pasta.

5 Drain the clams and reserve the liquid. Set the clams and their liquid aside.

6 In the same pan, heat the remaining oil with the garlic over a low heat for 3 minutes, then add the clams and strain the reserved liquid over.

7 Mix everything together and bring to the boil, then cover and take off the heat.

8 Add the pasta to the pan of salted boiling water and stir. Return to the boil and cook according to the pack instructions until al dente.

9 Drain the pasta and return it to the pan.

10 Pour the clams and liquid over the pasta and toss everything together. Add the parsley and plenty of freshly ground black pepper. Toss again and transfer to a warmed platter or bowl. Serve immediately.

VARIATION

This classic recipe can also be made with a tomato-based sauce, though it does make for a very different kind of dish. Use the same ingredients as here, but shell the clams and add a 400g/14oz can of tomatoes or passata (bottled strained tomatoes) to give the sauce a deep, sweet richness.

PER PORTION Energy 629kcal/2651kJ; Protein 40.3g; Carbohydrate 77.7g, of which sugars 3.6g; Fat 19.5g, of which saturates 2.9g; Cholesterol 117mg; Calcium 177mg; Fibre 3.5g; Sodium 210mg.

SPAGHETTI WITH DRIED FISH ROE
SPAGHETTI CON LA BOTTARGA

Bottarga is one of Sardinia's most important ingredients. It consists of tightly packed dried fish roe, which can be red mullet, grey mullet, tuna or other fish. The bottarga is often carefully sliced in transparent shavings over the finished dish with the same ceremony that is afforded to truffles in other regions of Italy. Cheaper, ready-grated bottarga is also available and can be bought in jars or sachets.

1 Bring a large pan of lightly salted water to a rolling boil. Add the spaghetti and stir. Return to the boil and cook for 8 minutes or according to the pack instructions until al dente. Drain and return to the pan, reserving some pasta water.

2 Meanwhile, grate the bottarga finely. Heat the oil in a large pan and fry the garlic for 5 minutes, or until golden, then take the pan off the heat.

3 Discard the garlic and add two-thirds of the bottarga to the pan with 25ml/1½ tbsp parsley.

4 Add plenty of ground black pepper and a ladleful of reserved water from the pasta pan, then stir to reduce the contents of the pan to a smooth cream.

5 Transfer the spaghetti to the pan with the bottarga sauce. Mix together thoroughly, adding a little more of the pasta water if the mixture appears to be drying out.

6 Divide the dressed pasta among four warmed plates, sprinkle with the remaining bottarga and parsley, and serve immediately.

SERVES 4

400g/14oz spaghetti
90g/3½oz bottarga, in a solid piece
75ml/5 tbsp olive oil
1 garlic clove, halved
30ml/2 tbsp chopped fresh flat leaf parsley
ground black pepper

PER PORTION Energy 493kcal/2077kJ; Protein 17.2g; Carbohydrate 74.4g, of which sugars 3.5g; Fat 16.1g, of which saturates 2.2g; Cholesterol 74mg; Calcium 48mg; Fibre 3.4g; Sodium 31mg.

SERVES 4

500g/1¼lb squid, cleaned and sliced into rings, the tentacles cut into sections (see Cook's Tip)
50ml/2fl oz/¼ cup olive oil
4 garlic cloves, crushed
1 salted anchovy, boned, rinsed and patted dry on kitchen paper
45ml/3 tbsp tomato purée (paste)
45ml/3 tbsp chopped fresh parsley
350g/13oz/1¾ cups risotto rice
½ dried red chilli, or to taste, crushed
sea salt

COOK'S TIP

Your fishmonger will prepare squid for you, but you can also do it yourself. Wash the squid carefully, rinsing off any ink. Holding the body firmly, pull away the head and tentacles. If the ink sac is still intact, remove it and discard. Pull out all the innards including the long transparent quill. Peel off and discard the thin purple skin on the body, but keep the two small side fins. Slice across the head just under the eyes, reserving the tentacles. Discard the rest of the head. Squeeze the tentacles at the head end to push out the round beak and discard. Rinse the pouch and tentacles well.

PER PORTION Energy 503kcal/2107kJ; Protein 26.8g; Carbohydrate 73.1g, of which sugars 1.7g; Fat 11.1g, of which saturates 1.7g; Cholesterol 281mg; Calcium 63mg; Fibre 0.9g; Sodium 198mg.

SQUID RISOTTO
RISOTTO CON LE SEPPIE

This is not the black and inky risotto of Venice, but the strong and garlicky version of the Lazio coastline. Sweet-tasting squid is a perfect backdrop for the intense flavours that typify the cuisine of the region, and it appears frequently on Lazio menus.

1 Dry the squid on kitchen paper. Heat the olive oil in a large pan and fry the garlic and anchovy together, stirring frequently, for 3 minutes, or until the garlic is just soft.

2 Add the tomato purée and the squid. Stir everything together, then simmer for 5 minutes.

3 Add enough cold water to cover generously. Do not add salt at this stage because it will turn the squid rubbery. Cover and simmer very slowly for about 2 hours, adding more water if necessary.

4 When the squid is completely tender, add the chopped parsley and the rice. Stir and continue to cook, stirring continuously, until the rice has absorbed the water.

5 Add a ladleful of boiling water and cook, stirring, as before. Add more boiling water, a ladleful at a time, only when the liquid in the pan has been absorbed into the rice. Continue in this way until the rice is cooked – it should be tender with a little bite in the centre.

6 Stir in salt and crushed chilli pepper to taste. Transfer to a platter to serve.

SARDINIAN SAFFRON RISOTTO
RISOTTO SARDO ALLO ZAFFERANO

This unusual risotto is from Sardinia, where small quantities of rice are grown, which means that risottos form part of the local traditional menu. Saffron also grows on this beautiful island, although, disappointingly, it seldom appears in the island's repertoire of recipes. On the occasions that it does, such as in this intensely flavoured and coloured dish, it really is superb. This is the only region of Italy where saffron is used in strands instead of powder.

1 Plunge the tomatoes into a bowl of boiling water for 30 seconds, then refresh them in cold water. Peel away the skins (they should come away easily) and chop them roughly. Set aside.

2 Heat the pork dripping, lard or pork belly in a pan, add the chopped onion and fry over a low heat for 5 minutes or until soft.

3 Add the pork cubes. Cook together for 10 minutes, adding the wine a little at a time, until the pork is browned all over.

4 Add the peeled, chopped tomatoes to the pan and mix everything together thoroughly.

5 Pour in the saffron and its soaking water. Continue to simmer gently, adding a little stock from time to time as necessary to keep it moist, for 20–30 minutes, or until the pork is falling into shreds.

6 Add the rice and stir until all the grains are coated with the liquid and are very hot.

7 Add a ladleful of stock and cook, stirring constantly, until the liquid has been absorbed into the rice.

8 Add more hot stock, a ladleful at a time, stirring continuously and allowing each ladleful of liquid to be absorbed before adding more each time. Continue in this way until the rice is cooked – it should be creamy and velvety, but the grains of rice should still be firm to the bite.

9 Season the risotto with salt and ground black pepper, then remove the pan from the heat.

10 Stir in the Pecorino cheese and cover the pan with a lid. Allow the risotto to rest, covered, for 2–3 minutes, then stir it again.

11 Serve the risotto immediately, in warmed bowls, sprinkled with extra Pecorino cheese and some ground black pepper.

SERVES 6

300g/11oz ripe tomatoes
75g/3oz pork dripping, lard or pork belly
1 large onion, finely chopped
300g/11oz pork, such as hand or shoulder, finely cubed
90ml/6 tbsp dry white wine
a pinch of saffron strands, soaked in a little warm water
1.5 litres/2½ pints/6¼ cups pork stock, simmering
500g/1¼lb/scant 3 cups risotto rice, such as arborio, carnaroli or vialone nano
50g/2oz/⅔ cup freshly grated Pecorino cheese, plus extra to serve
sea salt and ground black pepper

PER PORTION Energy 540kcal/2250kJ; Protein 20.9g; Carbohydrate 70.8g, of which sugars 3.5g; Fat 17.7g, of which saturates 7.6g; Cholesterol 51mg; Calcium 133mg; Fibre 1g; Sodium 132mg.

ROMAN SEMOLINA GNOCCHI
GNOCCHI ALLA ROMANA

This is a really soothing example of ultimate Roman comfort food. Circles of cooked semolina are luxuriously coated with butter and Parmesan cheese, then baked until golden. It makes a perfect supper dish for children, as it is delicate in flavour and sustaining. Alternatively, it can be served as a simple primo when preceding a very spicy or full-flavoured main course. Semolina gnocchi is also tasty served with a punchy green salad as a simple lunch dish.

SERVES 6

1 litre/1¾ pints/4 cups milk
250g/9oz/1⅓ cups semolina
2 egg yolks
100g/3¾oz/scant 1¼ cups freshly grated Parmesan cheese
100g/3¾oz/scant ½ cup unsalted butter, plus extra for greasing
a pinch of freshly grated nutmeg
sea salt and ground black pepper

1 Preheat the oven to 220°C/425°F/Gas 7 and grease a shallow, ovenproof dish.

2 Put the milk in a large pan and bring to the boil. Sprinkle in the semolina with one hand while whisking constantly with the other to prevent lumps forming.

3 Continue whisking until the mixture begins to thicken, then use a wooden spoon to stir constantly for about 10 minutes, or until the mixture begins to come away from the sides and the base of the pan, and forms a soft, rounded ball.

4 Remove the pan from the heat and stir in the egg yolks, half the Parmesan cheese and half the butter. Season to taste with the nutmeg, salt and ground black pepper.

5 Dampen a work surface lightly with cold water and pour out the semolina. Spread it out flat to a thickness of about 1cm/½in using a palette knife or metal spatula dipped in cold water.

6 Cut all the semolina into even circles using a 5cm/2in pastry (cookie) cutter or inverted tumbler.

7 Break up the scraps of left-over semolina and arrange them in a layer over the base of the dish – this means that none will be wasted.

8 Set aside about 25g/1oz/2 tbsp of the butter for melting at the end, then cover the semolina scraps with a few dots of butter and a sprinkling of grated Parmesan cheese.

9 Arrange a layer of slightly overlapping semolina circles on top of the semolina scraps, and cover these with a sprinkling of cheese and a few dots of butter as before. Continue in this way until all of the ingredients have been used up, except for the reserved butter.

10 Melt the reserved butter and trickle it over the top. Bake in the preheated oven for 15 minutes, or until golden. Serve immediately.

VARIATION

You can ring the changes and spice up this basic dish with the addition of extra ingredients. Try adding saffron, flaked cooked fish, chopped prosciutto, salami or Gorgonzola.

PER PORTION Energy 441kcal/1848kJ; Protein 17.6g; Carbohydrate 40.6g, of which sugars 8.3g; Fat 24.5g, of which saturates 14.6g; Cholesterol 132mg; Calcium 418mg; Fibre 0.9g; Sodium 406mg.

FISH AND SHELLFISH

PESCE E FRUTTI DI MARE

Sardinia, set in the sparkling Mediterranean Sea, has no shortage of fresh fish and shellfish on its menus. From meaty tuna loin to delicate sea bass, Sardinians cook their fish in a mixture of bold flavours, such as olives, onions and white wine vinegar. The stretch of Adriatic coastline shared by Abruzzo and Molise means that both these regions share a wealth of recipes that make the best of the local catch, including shellfish such as mussels, clams and prawns. Roman cuisine features some fish that are rarely used in other parts of the country, such as stingray and huss, that can be difficult to buy elsewhere. Campania features some of the most delicious fish and shellfish dishes of Italy, such as the light and fragrant fritto misto and the wonderfully simple, intriguingly named acqua pazza, or Crazy Water, to give it its English translation.

MUSSELS, CLAMS AND A CHUNKY FISH STEW

Despite the fact that the central regions enjoy access to the sea and therefore use both fish and shellfish extensively in their antipasti and pasta dishes, there are generally fewer recipes for fish main courses than you might expect. However, when central Italians do cook fish, they make sure it is as fresh as possible, then prepare it in the simplest way to make the very best of that freshness. Fish is often simply roasted, grilled or poached, with no embellishments other than salt and pepper, a squeeze of lemon and a drizzle of olive oil. Having said that, all these regions have time-honoured recipes for preparing fish.

Sardinia excels in the creation of lobster dishes, as this crustacean is plentiful in the crystal clear blue waters of the rocky coastline that surrounds most of the island. A lobster is the crowning glory of a typical Sardinian Fish Stew. The most highly prized fish throughout the whole country is the sea bass, known as spigola or branzino depending upon the region where it is caught, and Sardinia also boasts several wonderful recipes that make the most of this delicately flavoured fish.

In terms of shellfish, Lazio favours the small clams called arselle, shaped like an elongated triangle with a rounded end. These delicate and beautiful white and violet bivalves, with golden streaks radiating across the pattern on the shell, are sweet and delicious, and are very popular, although quite rare. For Neapolitans, and Campanians generally, the most prized clams are the vongola verace, or carpet clams, which are steamed open with white wine, garlic, chilli and parsley in the dish called sartu di vongole, or Sautéed Clams.

TUNA IN THE STYLE OF ALGHERO
TONNO AL ALGHERESE

This is a really unusual way of cooking a tuna loin, which is soaked then baked and served thickly sliced. The soaking keeps it extra moist. It is perfect to serve as an alternative to a meat joint, with roasted or boiled potatoes and a green vegetable.

1 Put the tuna into a large, deep bowl of cold water and add the vinegar. Leave to soak for 2 hours. Drain and pat dry on kitchen paper.

2 Heat the oil in a large, heavy frying pan, add the onion, celery and bay leaves, and fry gently for 5–10 minutes, until the onion is soft.

3 Add the tuna loin to the pan and cook gently, turning frequently, for 20 minutes.

4 Add the white wine to the pan and cook for 1–2 minutes to allow the alcohol to evaporate.

5 Add the olives and season with salt, then cover and simmer over a low heat for a further 10 minutes.

6 Thickly slice the tuna loin, then serve it on a warmed platter, with the sauce from the pan drizzled over.

SERVES 4 TO 6

1kg/2¼lb fresh tuna loin
100ml/3½fl oz/scant ½ cup white wine vinegar
100ml/3½fl oz/scant ½ cup extra virgin olive oil
1 onion, finely chopped
1 small celery stick, finely chopped
3 dried bay leaves
200ml/7fl oz/scant 1 cup dry white wine
30g/1¼oz/generous ¼ cup pitted black olives
sea salt

PER PORTION Energy 365kcal/1526kJ; Protein 40g; Carbohydrate 2.9g, of which sugars 2.1g; Fat 19.3g, of which saturates 3.6g; Cholesterol 47mg; Calcium 43mg; Fibre 0.7g; Sodium 196mg.

SERVES 4

150ml/¼ pint/⅔ cup extra virgin olive oil
1 onion, finely chopped
30ml/2 tbsp chopped fresh flat leaf parsley
4 medium sea bass, cleaned and scaled
175g/6oz/1 cup pitted black olives, roughly chopped
250ml/8fl oz/1 cup dry white wine, such as Vernaccia di Oristano
lemon wedges and boiled potatoes, to serve (optional)

PER PORTION Energy 483kcal/2004kJ; Protein 30.4g; Carbohydrate 4.7g, of which sugars 3.5g; Fat 33.8g, of which saturates 4.9g; Cholesterol 120mg; Calcium 265mg; Fibre 2.6g; Sodium 1096mg.

SEA BASS IN THE ORISTANO STYLE
ARANGIOLA A S'ORISTANESA

Black olives, onions and white wine are cooked with fresh sea bass in this lovely dish from Oristano in Sardinia. The wine traditionally used, Vernaccia di Oristano, is from this area, but any good dry white wine will work equally well.

1 In a frying pan large enough to hold all the fish, heat half the oil. Add the onion and parsley and fry over a medium heat until the onion is soft and golden.

2 Add the sea bass to the pan and baste them with the oil.

3 Add the olives and the wine, and cook over a high heat for 1 minute to evaporate the alcohol. Cover and cook for a further 5–10 minutes over a medium heat, until the fish is cooked through.

4 Serve the fish with the olive mixture on top, with lemon wedges and potatoes, if you like.

SERVES 4 TO 6

75ml/5 tbsp olive oil
1kg/2¼lb/4 cups canned tomatoes, drained, seeded and chopped
2 garlic cloves, chopped
60ml/4 tbsp chopped fresh parsley
10ml/2 tsp dried oregano
1 tiny dried, hot red chilli
5ml/1 tsp sea salt
1.5kg/3¼lb white fish fillets and/or steaks, such as cod or haddock
crusty bread, to serve (optional)

CRAZY WATER
ACQUA PAZZA

On the island of Ponza, the fishermen call any dish that is cooked in a lot of water all'acqua pazza – crazy water. Nobody really knows why, but the name has stuck, and cooking this way with lots of flavourings keeps the delicious taste of the fish intact.

1 Pour 1.5 litres/2½ pints/6¼ cups cold water into a large pan. Add the olive oil, tomatoes, garlic, herbs, chilli and salt. Stir well and bring to the boil.

2 Cover and simmer for 20 minutes.

3 Add the fish and cook for 5–10 minutes more, or until the fish is cooked through. This will depend on the size of the fillets.

4 Distribute among warmed dishes and serve, with crusty bread, if you like.

PER PORTION Energy 314kcal/1317kJ; Protein 47.2g; Carbohydrate 5.4g, of which sugars 5.4g; Fat 11.5g, of which saturates 1.7g; Cholesterol 115mg; Calcium 54mg; Fibre 2.2g; Sodium 168mg.

SARDINIAN FISH STEW
CASSOLA

All over Italy in all the small ports along the long coastline and on the islands, there are many recipes for creating sumptuous fish stews, soups and casseroles. This fish stew is a traditional recipe from the island of Sardinia and, like all the recipes for similar dishes, it relies on a wide selection of different kinds of fish and a few very simple ingredients to turn it into a memorable gastronomic experience. Here, dried and fresh red chilli gives the finished dish plenty of punch.

SERVES 4

120ml/4fl oz/½ cup extra virgin olive oil
1 onion, finely chopped
1 garlic clove, finely chopped, plus 1 garlic clove, halved
30ml/2 tbsp chopped fresh parsley
500g/1¼lb canned tomatoes, sieved (strained)
1 dried red chilli, chopped
1.5kg/3¼lb mixed fish, cut into even chunks, and a small whole lobster (optional)
4 thick slices coarse, crusty bread
1 fresh red chilli, whole
sea salt and ground black pepper

1 Heat the oil in a large pan, add the onion, the chopped garlic clove and the parsley, and fry for 5 minutes, until softened but not browned.

2 Add the tomatoes, a pinch of salt and the chopped chilli. Simmer for about 10 minutes, stirring gently.

3 Add the chunks of fish, starting with the thickest pieces and ending with the whole lobster, if using, basting with the sauce as you add each type of fish.

4 Add 200ml/7fl oz/scant 1 cup boiling water to the pan, cover and simmer over the lowest heat for about 1 hour.

5 Rub the slices of bread with the fresh chilli and the remaining garlic, then toast under a grill (broiler) for 1–2 minutes on each side, until golden and crispy.

6 Arrange the bread in a large serving bowl, and pour the fish stew over it, placing the lobster on top, if using. Serve immediately.

PER PORTION Energy 610kcal/2557kJ; Protein 65.8g; Carbohydrate 34.8g, of which sugars 9.7g; Fat 23.9g, of which saturates 3.5g; Cholesterol 150mg; Calcium 137mg; Fibre 3.7g; Sodium 473mg.

MIXED FRY-UP
FRITTO MISTO

Any variation of ingredients, in any quantity and in any combination, is acceptable for the classic Campanian dish fritto misto, but it's essential to have as many different ingredients as possible. This recipe uses a mixture of small fish, sliced vegetables and chunks of Italian cheeses, deep-fried in a simple batter. You will need either two deep-fryers or a large pan and a wok to cook this selection, and it is a good idea to make sure that your kitchen is well aired while you work.

SERVES 8

675g/1½lb small fish (such as whitebait) mixed with large raw prawns (shrimp)
1kg/2¼lb mixed vegetables, such as globe artichokes, very firm tomatoes, (bell) peppers, courgettes (zucchini), fennel, cut into even pieces about 4–6cm/1½–2½in
6 basil sprigs
6 sage sprigs
150g/5oz mozzarella, cut into even chunks
150g/5oz firm ricotta cheese, cut into even chunks
vegetable oil, for deep-frying
sea salt
4 lemons cut into wedges, to serve

FOR THE BATTER

5 eggs
50g/2oz/½ cup plain (all-purpose) flour
pinch of salt
750ml/1¼ pints/3 cups milk

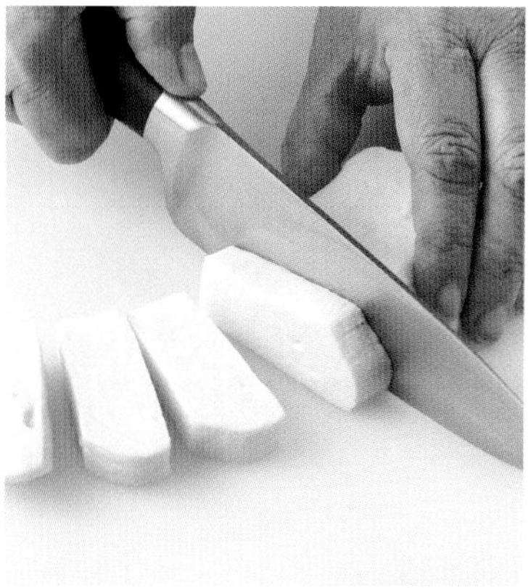

1 To make the batter, beat the eggs in a large bowl with a balloon whisk until well blended and smooth. Gradually add the flour and the salt, beating constantly. Then gradually pour in the milk, still beating. When you have a completely smooth batter, leave it to stand until required.

2 Make sure all the ingredients for deep-frying (the fish, vegetables, herbs and cheese) are as dry as possible.

3 Divide the batter equally into three large bowls. Put the fish into one, the vegetables into another and the herbs and cheese in the third. Submerge all of the ingredients in the batter and leave them to stand for about 30 minutes.

4 Pour the oil into two deep-fryers, deep pans or a pan and a wok. Lay out several layers of kitchen paper on to a large serving platter and place over a large pan of simmering water to keep everything warm without allowing the food to go soggy.

5 Heat the oil until a small cube of bread, dropped into the oil, sizzles instantly. The fish will be deep-fried in one pan, and all the other ingredients will be deep-fried in the second pan.

6 Quickly deep-fry the ingredients, in batches, turning them over in the oil after about 2 minutes and lifting them out with a slotted spoon as soon as they are golden and crisp. It is best to work quickly, in small batches to keep the oil at maximum heat, so that everything can cook as fast as possible.

7 Transfer the ingredients directly to the kitchen paper to drain, and sprinkle them with salt. Serve immediately on a warm platter with the lemon wedges.

PER PORTION Energy 618kcal/2566kJ; Protein 29.1g; Carbohydrate 14g, of which sugars 9.2g; Fat 50.1g, of which saturates 11.7g; Cholesterol 182mg; Calcium 223mg; Fibre 1.5g; Sodium 232mg.

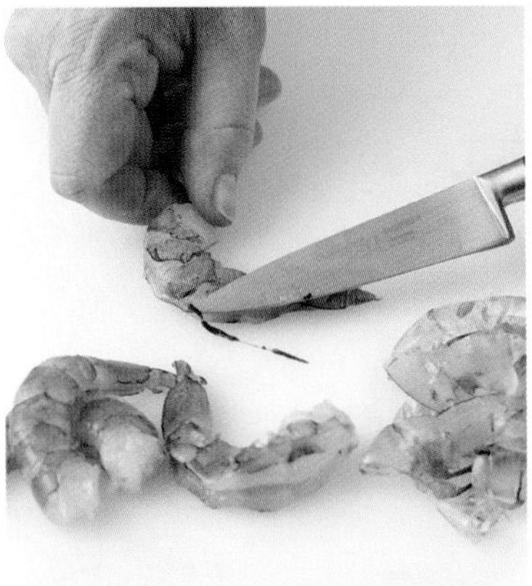

RICE RING MOULD WITH PRAWNS
TURBANTE DI RISO CON GAMBERI

Fresh prawns are cooked in two ways and served with a rice ring and a superbly creamy sauce that's full of the flavour of these tasty shellfish. It's the perfect dish for an impressive dinner-party main course. This recipe is from Campania, but it has a somewhat classic French style. This is typical of the recipes imported to the grand households of the area by the 19th-century French chefs who introduced their customs and traditions to the kitchens of the southern Italian aristocracy.

1 Set aside 30 prawns. Remove and reserve the shells from the others, then devein them (see Cook's Tip). Rinse well. Put the shells into a pan with the water, bouquet garni, 30ml/2 tbsp of the wine and the salt. Bring to the boil and simmer, covered, for 20 minutes. Strain into a clean pan, return to a simmer, and put the shells to one side.

2 Drop the shelled prawns into the strained stock. Blanch for 1 minute, remove with a slotted spoon and set aside. Simmer the stock for 10 minutes, then strain it again through a fine sieve (strainer). Put all the cooked shells into a food processor or blender and process or blend, with a little of the stock, to a creamy purée. Strain through muslin (cheesecloth) and set aside. Keep the stock hot.

3 Heat the oil and one-third of the butter in a large pan. Fry the onion and garlic for 10 minutes, gradually adding the remaining wine. Stir in half the parsley. Cook for 2 minutes, then add the 30 unshelled prawns. Fry over a high heat for 4 minutes, stirring. Transfer the prawns to a clean pan and place over a high heat. Pour over the cognac, ignite it, then immediately remove from the heat. Sprinkle the prawns with salt and keep them warm.

4 Add half the remaining butter to the pan in which the unshelled prawns were cooked. Heat it until it foams, then add the flour. Whisk thoroughly, then gradually add the stock, stirring. Simmer slowly, stirring, until smooth and thick. Sieve (strain) the sauce and return it to a low heat. Stir in the puréed prawn-shell cream, half the paprika, cream and remaining parsley. Pour half of this sauce over the shelled prawns and stir gently over a low heat.

5 Keep everything warm while you prepare the rice. Preheat the oven to 140°C/275°F/Gas 1. Lay a clean dish towel on a baking sheet. Spread the rice on top. Place in the oven for 10 minutes, then transfer to a bowl. Stir in the remaining butter. Grease the ring mould. Transfer the rice to the ring mould and place in the oven for 5 minutes.

6 Turn out the rice on to a serving dish. Pour the prawns in the sauce into the centre and arrange the unshelled prawns around the edges. Serve sprinkled with the rest of the paprika, and offer the remaining sauce separately.

SERVES 10

- 2.25kg/5lb large raw prawns (shrimp), with shells
- 1.5 litres/2½ pints/6¼ cups water
- 1 bouquet garni
- 175ml/6fl oz/¾ cup dry white wine
- 1.5ml/¼ tsp sea salt, plus extra to taste
- 30ml/2 tbsp olive oil
- 115g/4oz/½ cup unsalted butter, plus extra for greasing
- 1 onion, finely chopped
- 1 garlic clove, chopped
- 45ml/3 tbsp chopped fresh parsley
- 45ml/3 tbsp cognac
- 150g/5oz/1¼ cups plain (all-purpose) flour
- 5ml/1 tsp paprika, plus extra to serve
- 250ml/8fl oz/1 cup single (light) cream
- 800g/1¾lb/4 cups long grain rice, cooked in salted boiling water until just tender

COOK'S TIP

To devein the prawns, make a shallow cut down the centre of the curved back of each shelled prawn. Pull out the black vein with a cocktail stick (toothpick) or your fingers.

PER PORTION Energy 606kcal/2528kJ; Protein 27.8g; Carbohydrate 78.4g, of which sugars 2.6g; Fat 18.7g, of which saturates 10g; Cholesterol 110mg; Calcium 201mg; Fibre 1g; Sodium 1475mg.

DRUNKEN PRAWNS
GAMBERONI UBRIACHI

The region of Molise has few recipes to offer, but this is a delicious way of serving plump, juicy prawns, flavoured with basil, green pepper, garlic and cognac. It has to be eaten with the fingers for maximum enjoyment, so do supply finger bowls for guests.

1 Heat the olive oil in a large pan, add the garlic, onion, basil, parsley and green pepper, and fry over a medium heat, stirring frequently, until the pepper has softened.

2 Add the prawns and baste them with the oil. Cook until they are bright pink, then add the cognac and water. Simmer for 5 minutes, then serve, sprinkled with a few extra basil leaves.

SERVES 6

60ml/4 tbsp extra virgin olive oil
3 garlic cloves, finely chopped
$^{1}/_{2}$ onion, chopped
30ml/2 tbsp chopped basil, plus some extra basil leaves to serve
30ml/2 tbsp chopped fresh parsley
1 green (bell) pepper, cut into cubes
1kg/2$^{1}/_{4}$lb raw prawns (shrimp), with shells
120ml/4fl oz/$^{1}/_{2}$ cup cognac
120ml/4fl oz/$^{1}/_{2}$ cup cold water

PER PORTION Energy 192kcal/798kJ; Protein 15g; Carbohydrate 2.9g, of which sugars 2.5g; Fat 8.7g, of which saturates 1.4g; Cholesterol 52mg; Calcium 113mg; Fibre 1g; Sodium 1021mg.

SERVES 4 TO 6

1.5kg/3¼lb fresh clams, preferably carpet shell clams (see Cook's Tip)
50ml/2fl oz/¼ cup extra virgin olive oil
5 garlic cloves, chopped, plus 1 clove, halved
6 parsley sprigs, coarsely chopped
½–1 dried red chilli, coarsely chopped
150ml/¼ pint/⅔ cup dry white wine
4–6 slices crusty bread
sea salt and ground black pepper

COOK'S TIP

If possible, soak the clams overnight in several changes of salted water before cleaning them.

PER PORTION Energy 206kcal/870kJ; Protein 16.8g; Carbohydrate 20.4g, of which sugars 1g; Fat 5.2g, of which saturates 0.9g; Cholesterol 56mg; Calcium 124mg; Fibre 0.9g; Sodium 1194mg.

SAUTÉED CLAMS
SARTU DI VONGOLE

From Naples and Campania comes this simple and most delicious way to enjoy perfectly fresh clams. This style of cooking – superbly quick and easy, and using only a few top-quality, fresh ingredients – is absolutely typical of the cuisine of the area. The clams traditionally used for this classic dish are vongole veraci, known as carpet shell clams in English. They tend to be larger and juicier than the other varieties, but if you cannot get hold of them, any other clams are fine to use instead.

1 Scrub the clams in several changes of fresh water until the water is completely clear. Drain and set aside. Discard any clams that do not close tightly when tapped against a work surface.

2 Heat the olive oil in a pan large enough to take all the clams, and add the chopped garlic, parsley and chilli. Fry for 3 minutes, then add the clams, wine and seasoning.

3 Stir everything together thoroughly, then cover and leave to simmer, shaking the pan occasionally, for 6 minutes, or until the clams have opened up.

4 Meanwhile, toast the bread and rub one side of each slice with garlic. Remove the pan from the heat and discard any clams that remain closed. Pour the hot clams and their juices over the toasted garlic bread and serve.

FREGOLA WITH MUSSELS AND CLAMS
FREGOLA SARDA CON COZZE E VONGOLE

Rough, grainy-textured fregola pasta is a little like couscous and is becoming a popular choice in restaurants. It consists of fine beads of durum wheat pasta. Fregola is made by combining durum wheat flour and water – sometimes with the addition of saffron. It is then rolled, and the little balls of pasta are lightly toasted, which gives it a wonderful, nutty flavour. In this dish it is served with mussels and clams in a rich tomato sauce.

SERVES 6 TO 8

1kg/2¼lb mussels
1kg/2¼lb clams
3 garlic cloves, chopped
½ dried red chilli, chopped
60ml/4 tbsp chopped fresh flat leaf parsley
60ml/4 tbsp olive oil
1kg/2¼lb canned chopped tomatoes
250ml/8fl oz/1 cup dry white wine
1kg/2¼lb fregola
sea salt

1 Keeping the clams and mussels in separate bowls, scrub them thoroughly in several changes of fresh water until the water is completely clear. Scrape off any barnacles and pull off the 'beards' from the mussels. Drain. Discard any clams or mussels that do not close tightly when tapped against a work surface.

2 In a large pan over a low heat, fry the garlic, chilli and half the parsley in the oil for 3 minutes.

3 Add the mussels and cover the pan. Cook for 8 minutes, or until the mussels open. Remove the pan from the heat. Discard any mussels that remain closed. Remove the mussels from their shells, and strain and reserve the cooking liquid. Return the mussels and liquid to the pan.

4 Add the canned tomatoes, stir and lower the heat to simmer gently for 15 minutes.

5 Add the wine and season with salt. Cook for a further 5–10 minutes until the mussels are cooked and the liquid has reduced slightly.

6 Put the clams into a wide pan. Cover and cook them over a medium heat until they open. Discard any that remain closed. Strain the cooking liquid and add it to the pan with the mussels. Shell most of the clams, leaving a few in their shells, and add them to the pan.

7 Cook for a further 5 minutes, until the sauce is thick and glossy. Remove from the heat.

8 In another pan, boil the fregola in salted water for 8 minutes, or according to the pack instructions, then drain and add to the sauce with the remaining parsley. Stir well, then cover with a lid and leave to rest for 3 minutes before serving.

PER PORTION Energy 597kcal/2531kJ; Protein 27.7g; Carbohydrate 98.7g, of which sugars 8.35g; Fat 10.7g, of which saturates 1.6g; Cholesterol 45mg; Calcium 101mg; Fibre 5.2g; Sodium 589mg.

PEPPERED MUSSELS
IMPEPATA DI COZZE

This traditional way of serving mussels is from Naples. It is easy to prepare and very tasty, whether as an appetizer or main course. In the past, mussels were consumed only in the poorer south, but today they are celebrated as an important part of the menu.

SERVES 4 TO 6

60ml/4 tbsp extra virgin olive oil
2 garlic cloves, lightly crushed
1kg/2¼lb fresh mussels, cleaned (see Cook's Tip)
ground black pepper
wedges of lemon and slices of toasted, crusty Italian bread, to serve

1 Heat the oil and garlic in a large pan until hot and sizzling, then add the mussels and cover with a lid. Cook for 8 minutes, or until the mussels open. Shake the pan regularly during cooking. Discard any mussels that remain closed.

2 Take the pan off the heat and grind plenty of black pepper over the mussels (it should be obviously visible).

3 Serve them with lemon wedges and toasted crusty bread.

COOK'S TIP

Mussels need to be cleaned carefully. Scrub the shells with a stiff brush and rinse under cold running water. Discard any mussels that remain open after being sharply tapped. Scrape off any barnacles and remove the 'beards' by pulling from the bottom to the top to avoid tearing the flesh inside. Rinse well.

PER PORTION Energy 113kcal/469kJ; Protein 7.5g; Carbohydrate 1.5g, of which sugars 0g; Fat 8.5g, of which saturates 1.2g; Cholesterol 27mg; Calcium 23mg; Fibre 0g; Sodium 160mg.

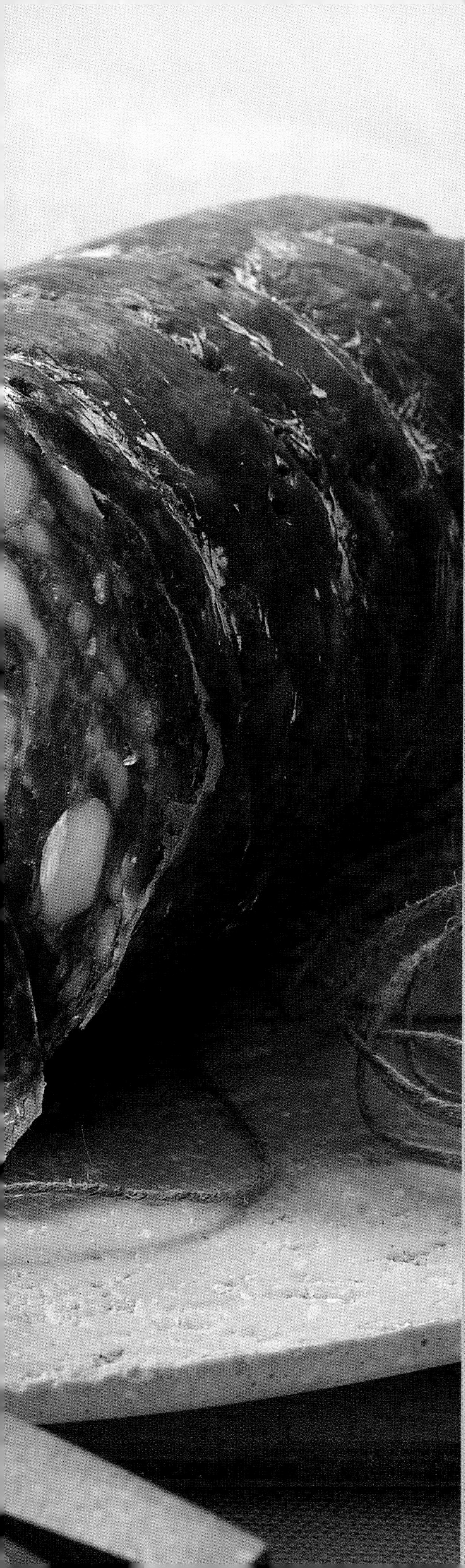

POULTRY AND MEAT
POLLAME E CARNE

Although not as important as pasta on the local menus, poultry and meat are certainly popular in this area of Italy. Chicken and turkey are common choices in Lazio, Campania, Molise, Abruzzo and Sardinia, as they are a perfect canvas for the famously strong flavours of these regions, creating really tasty dishes. Roman cuisine is known for its expertise in the preparation of offal dishes, making a feast out of the parts of animals that cooks in other regions simply discard. Most notable, perhaps, is the famous Roman Braised Oxtail, the stew of oxtail flavoured with plenty of celery and a rich tomato sauce. Lamb is sometimes called abbàcchio in Rome, and the famous dish abbàcchio alla Romana, or Roman Roast Lamb, is as Roman as the Colosseum. It is flavoured with bold ingredients such as red wine vinegar and anchovies, which help to cut the sweetness of the very young, tender lamb. Veal is used in a handful of recipes, where it lends its flavour to create rich sauces.

CHICKEN, LAMB AND ROMAN BRAISED OXTAIL

In Abruzzo, at the northern end of the sheep trail that winds its way from L'Aquila to Lecce, it is unsurprising to discover that lamb and mutton are the meats of choice. Molise, which lies halfway along the trail, also features lots of dishes using lamb in a variety of ways. In Abruzzo, piquant dried chilli is a favourite ingredient, and as a result, many of the local lamb or mutton dishes pack quite a punch.

Chicken and turkey appear on the menus, from the unusual Chicken Steeped in Myrtle from Sardinia to the famous Campanian dish Chicken Cacciatora, which is enjoyed all around the world today.

Generally speaking, apart from the very wide use of cured pork products such as pancetta or the lesser known guanciale, these regions tend not to use pork joints, chops or steaks very much. However, the most famous and symbolic dish of the island of Sardinia is actually the tender and delicious Porceddu – a whole, roasted suckling pig cooked slowly in an underground fire. Porchetta, or whole spit roasted sow, intensely flavoured with rosemary, pepper and garlic, is also popular throughout the whole of Lazio as a street food, sold from kiosks at the roadside or at the local markets.

The Campanian dish Genovese Onion Sauce, sometimes known as la Genovese, is a wonderful recipe that makes both a pasta and meat course – sweet onions are slowly cooked with a piece of veal, then the resulting sauce is served over pasta, and the meat carved for the main course. Also deservedly famous is the Roman veal dish saltimbocca alla Romana, which means 'jump in the mouth' – it is so delicious it can't bear to be left on the plate! Rome is also known for its fabulous preparation of offal, including age-old recipes for oxtail and kidneys.

CHICKEN STEEPED IN MYRTLE
GALLINA COL MIRTO

Using myrtle as a flavouring is common throughout the whole of Sardinian cuisine. It is a plant that produces small purple berries, which are harvested from November to January, and has fragrant leaves that are used in the preparation of many savoury meat and fish dishes. It is also made into the island's favourite liqueur, mirto. It may be difficult to get hold of outside of Sardinia, so try specialist Italian food stores. You will need a heatproof lidded container, such as a casserole or chicken brick.

1 Wash the chicken thoroughly and pat it dry with kitchen paper.

2 Put the onion in a deep pan with the carrot, celery and parsley, and cover with water. Season with salt. Cover and bring to the boil.

3 Once the stock is boiling, add the chicken. Cover and simmer for 1½ hours, or until the chicken is cooked through.

4 Line a large casserole or chicken brick with myrtle. Remove the chicken from the pan and transfer it to the container. Cover with more myrtle, put the lid on the top and leave the chicken to steam, off the heat, absorbing the flavour of the myrtle.

5 Leave the chicken in the myrtle-lined container until the next day, then remove from the casserole and serve cold.

SERVES 4 TO 6

1 medium oven-ready chicken, about 2.5kg/5½lb
1 large onion, halved
1 large carrot, halved
1 large celery stick, halved
a small bunch of flat leaf parsley
a large bunch of myrtle
sea salt

PER PORTION Energy 546kcal/2267kJ; Protein 51.7g; Carbohydrate 0g, of which sugars 0g; Fat 37.5g, of which saturates 10.4g; Cholesterol 275mg; Calcium 17mg; Fibre 0g; Sodium 188mg.

SERVES 6

50g/2oz dried porcini mushrooms, soaked in hot water for 20 minutes
90ml/6 tbsp olive oil
1 small carrot, chopped
1 celery stick, chopped
1 onion, chopped
1 garlic clove, chopped
1.2kg/2½lb chicken joints
1 bay leaf
5 juniper berries
175ml/6fl oz/¾ cup dry white wine
450g/1lb tomatoes, or 600g/1lb 6oz canned
750ml/1¼ pints/3 cups chicken stock
15ml/1 tbsp chopped fresh flat leaf parsley
sea salt and ground black pepper

PER PORTION Energy 405kcal/1686kJ; Protein 26g; Carbohydrate 4.3g, of which sugars 4g; Fat 29.7g, of which saturates 6.6g; Cholesterol 154mg; Calcium 26mg; Fibre 1.3g; Sodium 124mg.

CHICKEN CACCIATORA
POLLO ALLA CACCIATORA

Chicken cooked with tomatoes is a real classic among the best-loved Italian dishes. There are dozens of versions of the recipe for 'hunter's chicken', but this is the original one from Campania, flavoured with porcini mushrooms, wine and juniper berries. The variations on the basic recipe are very wide indeed. For some cooks this dish is just a plain chicken stewed in tomatoes with a little wine; others add olives or prawns, and some use completely different ingredients altogether.

1 Drain and chop the porcini mushrooms. Set aside. Heat the oil in a large pan and gently sauté the carrot, celery, onion and garlic for 15–20 minutes, or until tender, but not crisp.

2 Add the chicken, salt and pepper, bay leaf and juniper berries, and allow the chicken to brown over a high heat.

3 Add the wine, cook until it has evaporated, then add the mushrooms, tomatoes and stock.

4 Half-cover with a lid, then simmer for 45 minutes over a medium heat. When cooked through, remove from the heat, add the chopped parsley and arrange on a warm platter to serve.

STUFFED ROAST TURKEY IN THE MOLISE STYLE
TACCHINO RIPIENO ALLA MOLISANA

This is a superb recipe for a stuffed turkey from the little-known region of Molise. The food here has many similarities with its northern neighbour Abruzzo. However, Molise also shares some culinary traditions with Campania and Apulia – blending different Italian cooking traditions with its own local rustic ingredients. Classic accompaniments for the roast turkey include cabbage, braised onions, carrots or other seasonal vegetables. The same stuffing can also be used for chicken.

SERVES 8

4.5kg/10lb oven-ready turkey, with giblets
120ml/4fl oz/$^1/_2$ cup olive oil
$^1/_2$ onion, chopped
115g/4oz/2 cups fresh white breadcrumbs
2 eggs, beaten
45ml/3 tbsp freshly grated Pecorino cheese
30ml/2 tbsp pine nuts
30ml/2 tbsp currants, soaked in warm water for 15 minutes, then drained thoroughly
30ml/2 tbsp chopped fresh parsley
1.5ml/$^1/_4$ tsp freshly grated nutmeg
2 garlic cloves, crushed
15ml/1 tbsp finely chopped fresh rosemary leaves
15ml/1 tbsp black peppercorns
3 fresh sage leaves, chopped
75ml/5 tbsp dry white wine
sea salt and ground black pepper
stewed lentils or cannellini beans, to serve (see Cook's Tip)

1 Preheat the oven to 180°C/350°F/Gas 4. Wash the turkey inside and out, and dry it with kitchen paper. Trim and chop the giblets and put them into a pan with 15ml/1 tbsp olive oil and the chopped onion. Discard the neck.

2 Fry gently until the onion is soft and the meat is browned. Transfer to a bowl and leave to cool.

3 When cool, add the breadcrumbs, eggs, cheese, pine nuts, currants, parsley and nutmeg. Mix it all together very thoroughly and season to taste with salt and ground black pepper.

4 Add 15ml/1 tbsp olive oil, mix again and then use this mixture to stuff the turkey. Sew it closed tightly, using cook's string. Grease a roasting pan with about half the remaining oil.

5 Mix the garlic and rosemary into the remaining oil. Stir in the peppercorns and season with salt. Stir the sage leaves into the oil and add the white wine, then use about half of this mixture to brush all over the turkey. Reserve the rest of it to baste the turkey as it cooks.

6 Roast the turkey, basting frequently, for 3$^1/_2$ hours, or until the juices from the thickest part of the leg run clear and the bird is crisp and golden brown. Carve the turkey and serve it with stewed lentils or cannellini beans.

COOK'S TIP

To make tasty stewed pulses, gently sauté a clove of lightly crushed garlic with a little olive oil until pungent, then add 900g/2lb lentils, cannellini beans or other pulses (canned, or soaked and boiled until tender) and cook for 2–3 minutes. Add stock or water to cover and simmer until soft. Season with salt and pepper before serving.

PER PORTION Energy 839kcal/3513kJ; Protein 119.4g; Carbohydrate 14.7g, of which sugars 3.7g; Fat 33.2g, of which saturates 10.2g; Cholesterol 469mg; Calcium 157mg; Fibre 0.9g; Sodium 529mg.

SERVES 4

1kg/2¼lb very young, tender lamb on the bone
50ml/2fl oz/¼ cup olive oil
a knob (pat) of butter
1 lamb's kidney, cubed
250ml/8fl oz/1 cup water
350ml/12fl oz/1½ cups dry white wine or water
2 x 6cm/2½in rosemary sprigs
2 large preserved, salted anchovies, or 5 canned anchovy fillets in oil, drained
4 garlic cloves, peeled
60–75ml/4–5 tbsp red wine vinegar
sea salt and ground black pepper
steamed broccoli, to serve (optional)

ROMAN ROAST LAMB
ABBÀCCHIO ALLA ROMANA

The unexpected ingredients of salty anchovies and sour vinegar cut the sweetness of lamb to perfection in this springtime Roman speciality. With a hint of garlic and rosemary, it's the most delicious way to serve tender young lamb.

1 Wipe the meat carefully all over in case any bone shards remain, then cut into rough chunks about 7.5cm/3in square.

2 Set a wide, deep frying pan with a heavy base over a low heat. Add the oil and butter, and heat together for 5 minutes.

3 Add the kidney and meat chunks to the hot fat, browning them thoroughly all over. Season generously with salt and pepper, add the water, then lower the heat.

4 Cover and simmer for 45 minutes, occasionally adding a little water or wine and turning the meat from time to time.

5 Pound the leaves from the rosemary sprigs with the anchovies and garlic using a mortar and pestle. Stir in the vinegar and pour this mixture all over the meat. Stir thoroughly.

6 Simmer for 5 minutes, then serve immediately, with a green vegetable such as broccoli, if you like.

PER PORTION Energy 493kcal/2057kJ; Protein 38.5g; Carbohydrate 0.7g, of which sugars 0.6g; Fat 31.4g, of which saturates 12.1g; Cholesterol 183mg; Calcium 34mg; Fibre 0.1g; Sodium 522mg.

LAMB WITH CHEESE AND EGG
AGNELLO CACIO E UOVA

In this recipe from the region of the Abruzzo, cheese and eggs are beaten together with lemon juice to create a rich sauce to accompany the lamb. It is often served as part of the Easter feast in some parts of the south, and the ingredients are chosen as symbols of this important time in the Christian calendar. The primary ingredients are lamb, symbolic of the sacrifice of God's son; eggs, representing rebirth and the resurrection of Jesus; and vegetables, celebrating the return of the fertility of spring.

SERVES 4 TO 6

1 medium leg of lamb, about 2.25kg/5lb, boned
75ml/5 tbsp extra virgin olive oil
3 garlic cloves, coarsely chopped
a sprig of rosemary
250ml/8fl oz/1 cup dry white wine
90ml/6 tbsp freshly grated Pecorino cheese
4 eggs, beaten
juice of 1 lemon
30ml/2 tbsp chopped fresh flat leaf parsley
sea salt and ground black pepper
boiled potatoes and roasted red (bell) peppers, to serve (optional)

1 Cut the lamb into 2.5cm/1in chunks. Heat the oil in a large pan and add the garlic and the rosemary. Add the lamb and brown all over in the oil, gradually adding the white wine and using it to baste the meat.

2 Cover and simmer gently for 15 minutes, or until the lamb is cooked through. Remove the pan from the heat and discard the rosemary.

3 Beat the cheese and eggs together and add the lemon juice. Season with salt and pepper and pour this mixture over the lamb.

4 Return the pan to the heat and cook over a medium heat for 8 minutes, or until the eggs have set. Sprinkle with a little chopped parsley and serve, accompanied by boiled potatoes and roasted red peppers, if you like.

PER PORTION Energy 792kcal/3299kJ; Protein 63.3g; Carbohydrate 0.5g, of which sugars 0.4g; Fat 57g, of which saturates 20.9g; Cholesterol 333mg; Calcium 238mg; Fibre 0.4g; Sodium 702mg.

MUSHROOM AND MEAT SARDINIAN IMPANADAS
IMPANADAS DI FUNGHI E CARNI MISTE

This is a typical recipe from Sardinia, and is not to be confused with the well-known Argentinian dish called empanadas. Pastry fritters are filled with cooked meat, porcini mushrooms, sun-dried tomatoes, peas, onion and garlic, then deep-fried. The fritters can be made in a variety of different sizes, and using all kinds of ingredients, including grated Pecorino cheese, cured meats, or fresh fish – they work particularly well with small eels.

1 First, make the pastry. Rub the butter into the flour, with 1.5ml/¼ tsp salt, using your fingers or a pastry (cookie) cutter until it resembles fine breadcrumbs.

2 Sprinkle over 45ml/3 tbsp cold water. Using a fork, stir to just bind the dough together, adding more water as necessary, 15ml/1 tbsp at a time.

3 Using your hands, gather it together into a ball and put into a plastic bag or wrap it in clear film (plastic wrap). Chill the pastry for 30 minutes.

4 Place the porcini mushrooms in a small bowl and cover with warm water. Leave to soak for 30 minutes, then drain and rinse them well.

5 Melt the unsalted butter in a large pan and add the chopped onion, garlic, drained mushrooms, peas and sun-dried tomatoes. Cook for 10 minutes over a medium heat, or until the peas are tender.

6 Stir in the chopped, cooked meat and mix together. Season with salt and pepper, and allow the mixture to cool.

7 Roll out the pastry thinly on a floured surface and cut into circles using a 10cm/4in pastry (cookie) cutter.

8 Put a spoonful of the filling mixture in the centre of half the pastry circles. Use the other half of the circles (that don't have filling in them) to place on top, forming a lid. Seal the edges with your fingers, using a little beaten egg to make it stick.

9 Heat the oil until a small piece of the pastry, dropped into the oil, sizzles instantly. Fry the impanadas in batches until crisp and golden.

10 Carefully remove the impanadas using a slotted spoon and drain them on kitchen paper. Serve them piping hot.

SERVES 6

200g/7oz/scant 1 cup butter, cubed
400g/14oz plain (all-purpose) flour, plus extra for dusting
50g/2oz/1 cup dried porcini mushrooms
25g/1oz/2 tbsp unsalted butter
1 large onion, finely chopped
3 garlic cloves, finely chopped
45ml/3 tbsp fresh or frozen peas, thawed if frozen
5 sun-dried tomatoes, chopped
200g/7oz cooked meat (beef, lamb, pork or veal), finely chopped
1 small egg, beaten
vegetable oil, for deep-frying
sea salt and ground black pepper

COOK'S TIP

If you have not got time to make your own shortcrust pastry, you can use 500g/1¼lb ready-made shortcrust pastry, thawed if frozen. Begin the recipe at step 4.

PER PORTION Energy 672kcal/2795kJ; Protein 15.2g; Carbohydrate 49.2g, of which sugars 3.5g; Fat 47.4g, of which saturates 5.2g; Cholesterol 61mg; Calcium 101mg; Fibre 2.8g; Sodium 467mg.

SERVES 4 TO 6

2kg/4½lb brown onions, sliced
1 celery stick, chopped
200ml/7fl oz/scant 1 cup extra virgin olive oil
30ml/2 tbsp unsalted butter
1.5kg/3¼lb stewing veal in one single piece, tied into shape with cook's string to fit the pan
sea salt
large pasta shapes, such as sciaffettoni, and grated Parmesan cheese, to serve

GENOVESE ONION SAUCE
SALSA GENOVESE ALLA NAPOLETANA

The origin of this Neapolitan dish is still a mystery. It is a purée of the sweetest onions, cooked until browned and very soft, and flavoured with meat. One legend links the sauce to the chefs of the Genovese merchants living in Naples during the 16th century. When the merchants returned to Genoa, some of their chefs remained in Naples, selling food to the public. The sauce that was to become known as la Genovese was their speciality. The meat should be served as a second course, with a little of the sauce, after the pasta dish with the onion sauce. Sometimes the meat is omitted from the recipe altogether, and pasta served with the sauce made only with the onions is called a finta Genovese (fake Genovese).

1 Put the onions and celery into a deep pan, large enough to take the piece of meat. Add the oil and butter, and season with salt.

2 Lay the meat in the pan, add cold water to cover, then bring to the boil. Reduce the heat and simmer very slowly for 4 hours, stirring often and adding more water as required.

3 After this time, the meat should be very tender, and the onions should be completely brown and very soft. Serve most of the onion sauce over large pasta shapes as a primo, sprinkled with Parmesan cheese.

4 Serve the meat as a second course, sliced thinly with just a little of the sauce.

PER PORTION Energy 618kcal/2573kJ; Protein 56.8g; Carbohydrate 26.4g, of which sugars 18.7g; Fat 32.4g, of which saturates 5.8g; Cholesterol 210mg; Calcium 105mg; Fibre 4.7g; Sodium 288mg.

VEAL WITH SAGE, PROSCIUTTO AND MOZZARELLA
SALTIMBOCCA ALLA ROMANA

Although veal for saltimbocca is sometimes served rolled up, like a beef olive, the original recipe from Rome calls for it to be flat, with mozzarella melting on top, sealed in by a lightly fried slice of prosciutto. Fresh and fragrant sage tucked between the layers and added to the butter for frying is an essential part of the dish, as is the generous glug of dry white wine. Use Frascati, if you can get hold of it, to continue the Roman theme. Chicken or turkey breast can be cooked in this way too.

SERVES 4

8 thin veal escalopes (US scallops), about 115g/4oz each, trimmed
250g/9oz mozzarella
8 slices prosciutto crudo
16 fresh sage leaves
15ml/1 tbsp plain (all-purpose) flour
30ml/2 tbsp unsalted butter
120ml/4fl oz/$^1/_2$ cup dry white wine
sea salt and ground black pepper

1 Put the escalopes between two sheets of clear film (plastic wrap) or baking parchment and beat with a meat mallet or rolling pin until about 3mm/⅛in thick.

2 Cover each slice of meat with a slice of mozzarella and prosciutto, slipping a sage leaf between the meat and the mozzarella. Dredge the underneath of each saltimbocca in the flour to just coat.

3 Melt the butter in a large frying pan with the remaining sage leaves. Lay the escalopes, covered side down, in the pan to quickly seal the prosciutto to the meat with the cheese.

4 Turn and fry the other side until opaque, making sure the butter does not colour and burn. Season to taste.

5 Cover the pan and continue to cook gently for just 1–2 minutes, or until the cheese is oozing out from under the ham and the saltimbocca is cooked all the way through. Transfer to a serving platter and keep warm.

6 Pour the wine into the pan and boil quickly, stirring and scraping the juices from the base of the pan, for 3 minutes to create the sauce.

7 Pour the sauce over the meat and serve.

PER PORTION Energy 540kcal/2266kJ; Protein 73.4g; Carbohydrate 3.4g, of which sugars 0.5g; Fat 24g, of which saturates 14.4g; Cholesterol 198mg; Calcium 247mg; Fibre 0.1g; Sodium 752mg.

ROMAN BRAISED OXTAIL
CODA ALLA VACCINARA

For thousands of years, until the Second World War, teams of oxen ploughed fields and pulled loads in the countryside around Rome. When they could no longer work, they were slaughtered and their skins became leather, their horns a variety of accessories and their meat was cooked in stews. The people whose jobs were to slaughter, butcher and skin the oxen were paid with skins, unwanted offal and other parts of the animal – including the oxtails. This created a style of cooking that is closely associated with the Roman neighbourhood where the slaughterhouse and tanneries were located – Testaccio. Nowadays, it is a trendy area, but the traditions remain, and the local restaurants still serve these old Roman dishes, using the humblest meats.

1 Bring a large pan of water to the boil and add the chunks of oxtail and cheek. As soon as the water comes back to the boil, remove the meat using a slotted spoon. Set it aside to cool.

2 Put the chopped pork belly or bacon into a separate pan with the carrot, celery stick, onion and garlic. Fry gently together for 10 minutes, stirring frequently.

3 Add the oxtail and cheek, and brown it thoroughly all over. Season with salt and a generous pinch of crushed dried red chilli.

4 Add half the wine and cook for 1 minute to evaporate the alcohol.

5 Pour in the diluted tomato purée and stir. Cover with a lid, and simmer for 1 hour.

6 Add the remaining wine and cook, uncovered, for 2–3 minutes to evaporate the alcohol. Cover and simmer for 3 hours more.

7 Stir in the diced celery and cook slowly for a further 30 minutes. Transfer the finished dish to a platter and serve immediately.

SERVES 6

- 1 oxtail and 1 ox cheek, 2.5kg/5½lb total weight, cut into large chunks
- 200g/7oz pork belly or bacon, finely chopped
- 1 large carrot, very finely chopped
- 1 celery stick, very finely chopped, plus 5 celery sticks, diced
- 1 onion, very finely chopped
- 2 garlic cloves, very finely chopped
- a large pinch of crushed dried red chilli
- 250ml/8fl oz/1 cup dry white wine
- 45ml/3 tbsp tomato purée (paste) diluted in 500ml/17fl oz/generous 2 cups warm water
- sea salt and ground black pepper

PER PORTION Energy 395kcal/1646kJ; Protein 32.4g; Carbohydrate 2.8g, of which sugars 2.7g; Fat 25.4g, of which saturates 10g; Cholesterol 124mg; Calcium 39mg; Fibre 0.9g; Sodium 213mg.

SERVES 4 TO 6

500g/1¼lb calf's kidneys, trimmed
500g/1¼lb ripe tomatoes
15ml/1 tbsp lard or white cooking fat
1 large onion, finely sliced
45ml/3 tbsp dry red wine
sea salt and ground black pepper
30ml/2 tbsp chopped fresh parsley, to garnish

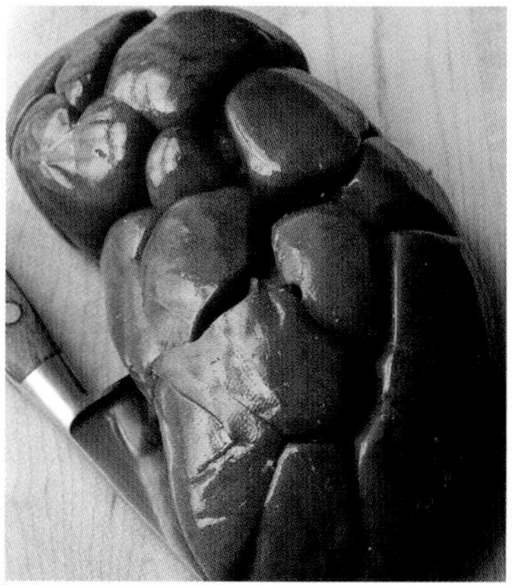

PER PORTION Energy 131kcal/551kJ; Protein 14.3g; Carbohydrate 6.6g, of which sugars 5.4g; Fat 5g, of which saturates 2g; Cholesterol 336mg; Calcium 27mg; Fibre 1.5g; Sodium 160mg.

ROMAN STEWED KIDNEYS
ROGNONE IN UMIDO

Offal is an important aspect of Roman cuisine, and it crops up in many different recipes. It is important to wash the kidneys carefully in several changes of cold water before using, in order to remove any trace of ammonia flavour.

1 Slice the kidneys and put them into a pan over a low heat. Cover with a lid and cook for 10 minutes to remove the bitter water.

2 Remove the kidneys and transfer to a sieve (strainer) set over the sink. Leave to drain for at least 20 minutes.

3 Meanwhile, plunge the tomatoes into boiling water for 30 seconds, then refresh in cold water. Peel away the skins and remove the seeds. Chop them roughly.

4 In a large pan, melt the lard or fat and gently fry the onion for 10 minutes, until soft.

5 Add the tomatoes. Simmer, covered, for 15 minutes, until the tomatoes start to fall apart.

6 Add the kidneys and stir together. Add the wine and cook for 1 minute to evaporate the alcohol. Add salt and pepper and stir again.

7 Simmer for 5 minutes, then transfer to a warm serving dish and sprinkle with the parsley.

VEGETABLES, EGGS AND CHEESE

VERDURE, UOVA E FORMAGGIO

La Campagna Romana, the vast plain of Lazio that rolls and dips from Rome to Circeo, is intersected by ditches and hills, and has been lauded since the time of ancient Rome as a wonderfully fertile area for the production of delicious vegetables and fruits. Similarly, the rich volcanic soil around Vesuvius in Campania has also been well known for centuries as an ideal place to grow certain vegetables, such as the pale pink tomato favoured locally for making the Caprese salad. Abruzzo, being more mountainous, is generally less favourable for growing such crops, although it is perfect for the production of fabulous lentils, especially around the town of Castelluccio. Nutritious eggs are used to create light lunches and local cheeses are celebrated in a wealth of recipes.

SUN-RIPENED TOMATOES AND RICOTTA FRITTERS

The huge variety of locally grown vegetables and the range of highly nutritious beans and lentils are combined with cheese and sometimes eggs to create some wonderful dishes. Campania is the most important region in Italy with regard to the production of tomatoes. This is where the fruit was first presented at court after its discovery in the New World, and where almost two centuries later it finally began to be used as an ingredient for cooking. It is probably the proximity to Vesuvius, and hence the rich soil full of sulphur, and the bright sunlight reflected off the sea that make the tomatoes grown in this region taste so wonderful.

Despite the fact that milk and butter are not common ingredients in these regions, there are several different kinds of cheese that are highly prized and much loved. Pecorino, made from ewe's milk, and used both as a table cheese and as a hard grating cheese, is widely eaten throughout the area, often in preference to milder Parmesan. Most notable are the well-known and very strong, peppery Pecorino Romano with its black rind, and the often more gentle Pecorino Sardo. There are enormous variations in the strength of these cheeses, depending upon both the producer and the length of time the cheese has been allowed to mature. A secondary cheese, from the same batch of milk that created Pecorino, is ricotta, which is made using the curds left after the Pecorino is drained and which are then re-boiled: the word ricotta means 'cooked again'.

Eggs have their place not just as an inexpensive and sustaining ingredient, but also as a feature in many recipes, such as Baked Eggs with Tomatoes, from Lazio.

SERVES 4

500g/1¼lb/2½ cups canned tomatoes, seeded and chopped
45ml/3 tbsp olive oil
8 eggs
sea salt and ground black pepper
green salad, to serve (optional)

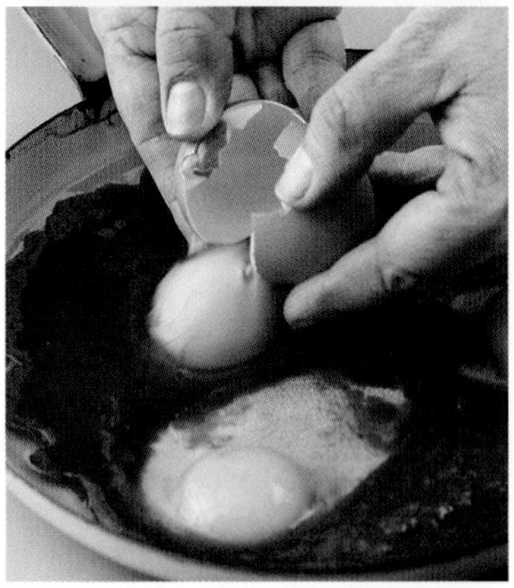

BAKED EGGS WITH TOMATOES
UOVA AL TEGAMINO CON POMODORO

This really is a delightfully simple dish, which comes from Lazio. Serve it with plenty of crusty bread and a dressed green salad. If you like, you can add some chopped canned anchovy fillets or capers to the tomato sauce after straining, which will give a more robust-tasting dish. Alternatively, you could sprinkle the finished dish with a generous pinch of dried oregano or torn fresh basil leaves. This recipe will make four servings, but if you are serving it as an appetizer, it will make enough for eight people.

1 Preheat the oven to 200°C/400°F/Gas 6. Put the tomatoes into a pan with 30ml/2 tbsp water and 2 pinches of salt. Cover and simmer slowly for 30 minutes, stirring occasionally.

2 Push the tomato sauce through a sieve (strainer) using the back of a spoon.

3 Pour the oil into an ovenproof dish and pour the sauce on top of the oil. Break the eggs on top of the sauce and sprinkle with pepper.

4 Bake for 5 minutes, or until the eggs are just set but the yolks are still runny. Serve immediately, with a green salad, if you like.

PER PORTION Energy 243kcal/1008kJ; Protein 13.4g; Carbohydrate 3.9g, of which sugars 3.9g; Fat 19.7g, of which saturates 4.4g; Cholesterol 381mg; Calcium 66mg; Fibre 1.3g; Sodium 151mg.

POTATO, ONION AND TOMATO BAKE
TERRINA DI PATATE, CIPOLLE E POMODORO

The humble potato is sliced and layered with red onion, tomato and breadcrumbs to make a very easy dish from Abruzzo that is full of flavour. It's ideal for a light lunch, served with a big salad and some crusty, warm garlic bread.

SERVES 4

4 large potatoes, peeled
25ml/1 1/2 tbsp dried oregano
135ml/9 tbsp olive oil, plus extra for greasing
60ml/4 tbsp fresh white breadcrumbs
3 very large, ripe tomatoes, such as beefsteak or marmande, sliced
3 red onions, thinly sliced into rings
sea salt and ground black pepper

1 Boil the potatoes for 4 minutes, then drain and slice into thin discs.

2 Grease a shallow ovenproof dish (large enough to hold all the vegetables) with olive oil.

3 Arrange a layer of potatoes on the bottom of the dish. Sprinkle with oregano, a little olive oil and a few pinches of breadcrumbs, then season with salt and pepper.

4 Cover with a layer of tomatoes and a layer of onions, topped with seasoning, oil and breadcrumbs as before.

5 Repeat the layers until all the vegetables have been used up, finishing with a generous coating of breadcrumbs. Leave to stand while you preheat the oven to 180°C/350°F/Gas 4.

6 Bake for 30 minutes, or until the top is browned and crisp. Serve warm.

PER PORTION Energy 473kcal/1978kJ; Protein 7.2g; Carbohydrate 55.6g, of which sugars 12.5g; Fat 26.2g, of which saturates 3.8g; Cholesterol 0mg; Calcium 65mg; Fibre 5g; Sodium 150mg.

POTATOES WITH LENTILS
PATATE E LENTICCHIE

Here is a typical, simple rustic dish from the Abruzzo region that is bursting with flavour. A good helping of olive oil gives richness to the combination of lentils and vegetables – and you can also add some pancetta or bacon. Serve this as an accompaniment to a game stew or chicken casserole, or enjoy it on its own with some crusty bread and a good bottle of red wine. Some types of lentils need to be soaked before they are cooked, so make sure you check the packet instructions.

1 Rinse the lentils, then put them in a pan of water to cover. Bring to the boil and cook for 5 minutes. Drain and rinse again.

2 Return the lentils to the pan, and add fresh cold water to just cover. Simmer for 15 minutes. Set aside.

3 Heat the oil in a separate pan, and gently fry the celery, carrot, onion, garlic, pancetta or bacon, if using, and rosemary, until softened and the fat in the meat begins to run.

4 Add the lentils with their cooking liquid and stir thoroughly. Season generously with salt and pepper. Cover and simmer slowly for 30 minutes, stirring frequently.

5 Add the potatoes and stock and continue to cook, uncovered, until the potatoes are tender all the way through.

6 Adjust the seasoning to taste as necessary and serve immediately, with a tomato salad, if you like.

SERVES 4

150g/5oz/$^2/_3$ cup brown or green lentils
75ml/5 tbsp olive oil
1 celery stick, coarsely chopped
1 large carrot, chopped
1 large onion, chopped
2 garlic cloves, chopped
3 rashers (strips) pancetta, or streaky (fatty) bacon, chopped (optional)
10cm/4in rosemary sprig
4 or 5 medium potatoes, cubed
250ml/8fl oz/1 cup chicken or meat stock
sea salt and ground black pepper
tomato salad, to serve (optional)

COOK'S TIP

Also excellent served cold, with salad, cheese and bread.

PER PORTION Energy 405kcal/1705kJ; Protein 13.3g; Carbohydrate 57.3g, of which sugars 5.7g; Fat 15.2g, of which saturates 2.3g; Cholesterol 0mg; Calcium 52mg; Fibre 6.3g; Sodium 39mg.

SERVES 4

300g/11oz/1 2/3 cups dried cannellini beans, soaked overnight
1 celery stick, quartered
500g/1 1/4lb ripe tomatoes
30ml/2 tbsp chopped fresh parsley, plus extra to garnish
2–3 garlic cloves, chopped
135ml/9 tbsp olive oil
2.5ml/1/2 tsp dried oregano
8 thin slices stale ciabatta
sea salt and ground black pepper

COOK'S TIPS

- If you are able to find fresh cannellini beans in their pods, you will need 1.2kg/2 1/2lb. Soak them overnight as for dried beans, then cook them for about 20 minutes, until soft, at step 2.
- The beans should be extremely mushy; the dish should have the consistency of thick soup. If necessary, add a little boiling water.

PER PORTION Energy 444kcal/1858kJ; Protein 17.5g; Carbohydrate 37g, of which sugars 5.8g; Fat 26.2g, of which saturates 3.8g; Cholesterol 0mg; Calcium 87mg; Fibre 13.1g; Sodium 29mg.

STEWED BEANS WITH BREAD
FAGIOLI ALLA MARUZZARA

In Campania, this dish uses fresh white cannellini beans, but they are difficult to get hold of outside of Italy. Dried beans, as used here, will work equally well, but remember that they will need to be soaked overnight before they are cooked.

1 Drain and rinse the beans, then place in a pan. Cover with water and bring to the boil. Boil for 5 minutes, then drain and rinse well.

2 Return to the pan and cover with plenty of water. Bring to the boil. Cover and simmer slowly for 10 minutes. Add the celery and continue to simmer for a further 30 minutes.

3 Meanwhile, plunge the tomatoes into boiling water for 30 seconds, then refresh in cold water.

4 Peel the skins from the tomatoes and discard. Halve them, and remove and discard the seeds. Chop the tomatoes coarsely.

5 Add the tomatoes to the pan with the parsley, garlic, oil and oregano. Season generously and cook for a further 15 minutes; the beans should be mushy.

6 Divide the ciabatta among four soup plates and pour the beans over the bread. Serve, sprinkled with chopped parsley.

SERVES 4

4 yellow (bell) peppers
60ml/4 tbsp olive oil
2 garlic cloves, sliced
15ml/1 tbsp tomato purée (paste)
7.5ml/1½ tsp salted capers, rinsed and chopped
3 anchovy fillets, preserved in oil, drained and chopped
sea salt
salad and bread, to serve (optional)

YELLOW PEPPERS WITH CAPERS
PEPERONI IN TEGLIA ALLA NAPOLETANA

This is one of those dishes that brings together the colours, flavours and textures of the food of southern Italy absolutely perfectly. The dish is best when eaten at room temperature, with lots of green salad, bread and chilled white wine.

1 Halve the peppers and remove the seeds and membranes. Cut each pepper into four pieces.

2 Heat the oil in a pan and fry the garlic until browned. Add the peppers. Dilute the tomato purée with 45ml/3 tbsp water and pour over the peppers.

3 Season with salt, then stir. Cover and simmer for 15–25 minutes, until the peppers are soft.

4 Mix the capers and anchovies together, then stir them into the cooked peppers. Cover and leave to stand for 3 minutes before serving warm with salad and bread. Alternatively, serve cold.

PER PORTION Energy 168kcal/696kJ; Protein 2.9g; Carbohydrate 11.7g, of which sugars 11.2g; Fat 12.5g, of which saturates 1.7g; Cholesterol 0mg; Calcium 27mg; Fibre 2.9g; Sodium 164mg.

AUBERGINES WITH TOMATO AND MOZZARELLA
MELANZANE ALLA PARMIGIANA

Many versions of this classic recipe exist all over the south of Italy, but the principle is always the same: layers of cooked aubergine with tomato sauce, basil and cheese, baked in the oven. It's a hearty dish, which tastes even better the next day.

SERVES 4

3 long aubergines (eggplants), cut into circles
45ml/3 tbsp extra virgin olive oil, plus extra for greasing
250ml/8fl oz/1 cup passata (bottled strained tomatoes)
115g/4oz mozzarella, sliced
200g/7oz Parmesan cheese, grated
15 fresh basil leaves, torn into shreds
sea salt and ground black pepper

1 Sprinkle the aubergine slices with salt and lay them in a colander. Put a plate on top and weight it down. Stand the colander in the sink for 1 hour to allow the bitter juices of the aubergines to drain away.

2 Rinse and pat the aubergine slices dry, then brush them lightly with oil. Use the extra oil to lightly grease four medium ramekins.

3 Heat the grill (broiler) to high and grill (broil) the aubergine slices until soft and lightly browned, turning them once.

4 Preheat the oven to 180°C/350°F/Gas 4. Put a little passata across the bottom of an ovenproof dish. Cover with a layer of aubergine slices.

5 Cover with a layer of mozzarella, a layer of passata, a sprinkling of Parmesan cheese and a few torn basil leaves.

6 Repeat the layers until the ingredients are used up, finishing with a thick layer of passata, topped with Parmesan cheese and basil. Bake for 40 minutes, or until golden. Leave to stand for 10 minutes before serving.

VARIATION

The aubergines can also be shallow fried in oil instead of grilling (broiling), and then used as above, from step 4.

PER PORTION Energy 407kcal/1693kJ; Protein 26.8g; Carbohydrate 5.2g, of which sugars 5g; Fat 31.2g, of which saturates 15.6g; Cholesterol 67mg; Calcium 724mg; Fibre 3.6g; Sodium 667mg.

COURGETTES WITH TOMATO AND MOZZARELLA
ZUCCHINE ALLA BELLA NAPOLI

In this dish, sliced courgettes are dusted in flour then quickly fried before being layered with tomato and mozzarella, and then baked. Although it is fairly labour intensive, the end result is delicious and the dish is lovely served either hot or cold.

1 Arrange the sliced courgettes on a platter, sprinkle with salt and stand it in the sink. Lift it up at one end so that the platter remains on a slant and allows the juices from the courgettes to seep out into the sink. Leave for 1 hour.

2 Meanwhile, heat the dripping or white cooking fat and olive oil in a large pan and fry the onion for about 10 minutes, until soft. Add the tomatoes, basil and oregano. Season with salt, then cover and simmer for 45 minutes.

3 Push the tomato sauce through a sieve (strainer) using the back of a spoon. Preheat the oven to 180°C/350°F/Gas 4.

4 Rinse and dry the courgettes on kitchen paper. Heat the sunflower oil in a large pan until a small piece of bread, dropped into the oil, sizzles instantly.

5 Dust the courgette slices lightly in flour, then fry them carefully in the hot oil, in batches, until lightly golden. Remove them with a slotted spoon and drain on kitchen paper. Set aside.

6 Arrange the courgettes, sauce and mozzarella in layers in a shallow ovenproof dish, finishing with a layer of tomato sauce.

7 Bake for 20 minutes and serve hot or cold.

SERVES 4

6 courgettes (zucchini), thinly sliced lengthways
50g/2oz dripping or white cooking fat
45ml/3 tbsp olive oil
1 very small onion, finely sliced
500g/1$\frac{1}{4}$lb ripe tomatoes, quartered and seeds removed
5 fresh basil leaves
2.5ml/$\frac{1}{2}$ tsp dried oregano
sunflower oil, for deep-frying
30ml/2 tbsp plain (all-purpose) flour
300g/11oz mozzarella, finely sliced
sea salt

PER PORTION Energy 649kcal/2682kJ; Protein 20.2g; Carbohydrate 15.4g, of which sugars 9.1g; Fat 56.6g, of which saturates 20.7g; Cholesterol 55mg; Calcium 357mg; Fibre 4g; Sodium 311mg.

SERVES 4

45ml/3 tbsp extra virgin olive oil, plus extra for greasing
4 slices slightly stale white bread
45ml/3 tbsp milk
2 scamorza, thinly sliced
sea salt and ground black pepper

SCAMORZA CROSTINI
CROSTINI CON LA SCAMORZA

An often underrated cheese, scamorza is made by allowing mozzarella to dry out so that it forms a thin rind on the outside. It is sometimes smoked, giving it a light brown skin and slightly woody flavour, which becomes more pronounced when it melts.

1 Preheat the oven to 180°C/350°F/Gas 4. Grease a shallow baking tray with oil.

2 Lay the slices of bread on the baking tray. Drizzle the bread with enough of the milk to moisten it.

3 Cover the bread with the sliced scamorza and sprinkle with the oil. Season with salt and plenty of pepper.

4 Bake for 10 minutes, until the bread is crisp and the cheese is bubbling. Serve immediately.

VARIATION

Try adding some chopped anchovy fillets, or topping with prosciutto crudo.

PER PORTION Energy 340kcal/1415kJ; Protein 16.7g; Carbohydrate 14.7g, of which sugars 1.3g; Fat 24.2g, of which saturates 11.7g; Cholesterol 44mg; Calcium 317mg; Fibre 0.4g; Sodium 452mg.

RICOTTA FRITTERS
CALZONCINI ABRUZZESI

These hearty little fritters from Abruzzo can be served as part of an antipasti selection or as a tasty cheesy snack at any time of day. Traditionally, they would be part of a great mound of deep-fried goodies such as artichoke hearts, scamorza cheese, cauliflower florets and many other delicious bits and pieces. This would be followed by the pasta course, the main course and then the desserts. Some feasts in the Abruzzo can begin at one o'clock and not finish until seven o'clock in the evening!

1 Put the ricotta cheese in a bowl and mix with the egg yolks, prosciutto, provolone and parsley, and season with salt and black pepper. Stir until the mixture has a smooth, even consistency. Set aside while you make the pastry.

2 To make the pastry, put the flour on to the work surface. Make a hole in the centre and break in the eggs. Add the lard, lemon juice and a pinch of salt.

3 Knead it all together until you have a smooth ball of dough.

4 Roll the dough out thinly on a floured surface and cut into 7.5cm/3in circles using a pastry (cookie) cutter.

5 Put a teaspoonful of the filling on one half of each circle, fold in half and seal tightly by pressing the prongs of a fork all the way around the open edge.

6 Heat the vegetable oil in a large pan or deep-fryer until a small piece of the pastry, dropped into the oil, sizzles instantly.

7 Slide the calzoncini into the oil, about four at a time, and fry them until puffy and golden.

8 Remove the calzoncini using a slotted spoon, drain on kitchen paper and keep them warm while you cook the rest. Serve them piping hot.

SERVES 6

300g/11oz/generous 1¼ cups ricotta cheese
2 egg yolks
115g/4oz prosciutto crudo, finely chopped
115g/4oz/1 cup coarsely grated provolone cheese
50g/2oz/1 cup chopped fresh parsley
vegetable oil, for deep-frying
sea salt and ground black pepper

FOR THE PASTRY

400g/14oz/3½ cups plain (all-purpose) flour, plus extra for dusting
2 eggs
115g/4oz/⅔ cup lard or white cooking fat
juice of I lemon
salt

PER PORTION Energy 737kcal/3071kJ; Protein 21.3g; Carbohydrate 53.8g, of which sugars 2.9g; Fat 50.1g, of which saturates 17.9g; Cholesterol 192mg; Calcium 198mg; Fibre 2.5g; Sodium 337mg.

di Capri

DESSERTS AND BAKING
DOLCI

In poorer areas like Molise and the more remote parts of Abruzzo, Lazio, Campania and Sardinia, the traditional preparation of something sweet, such as cakes, biscuits or a pudding, was a treat very much reserved to mark a special occasion or holy festival. Historically very few households would have been able to afford sugar, nuts, glacé (candied) fruit or honey, and fewer still would have possessed an oven. Many of the smaller communities, especially those far away from the larger cities, would have shared a communal oven for the baking of individual loaves of bread, so it would have been impractical to take up oven space with a cake or a batch of biscuits without the excuse of a special occasion. Many of the desserts in this chapter reflect this history by the simplicity of their ingredients and their imaginative use. It is also noticeable that many of the sweet recipes are specifically made for religious holidays, such as Easter and Christmas.

FRITTERS, COOKIES AND CHOCOLATE-TOPPED CAKES

The island of Sardinia has a collection of delicately decorated biscuits and pastries that are unique and pretty, but made using the simplest of ingredients. Sardinians like their pastries sweet and full of flavour, and they differ from town to town. Many feature almonds, which are grown on the island, candied orange peel or lemon zest, and often honey. Corbelozzo honey, from the arbutus blossom, is popular there too. It is made by bees that buzz among the abundant growth of wild arbutus, or strawberry trees, found throughout the island. Only slightly sweet, with a bitter tang and an almost minty flavour, it is often served with sebadas, which are fritters of puff-type pastry dough, stuffed with fresh, sweet sheep's milk cheese and then deep-fried before being drizzled generously with honey.

Campania's most famous dessert is the traditional pastiera, made in the springtime with soaked and boiled wheat to promote a good sowing season and ongoing fecundity throughout the year ahead. The pastiera is a typical dessert of the Easter period which, according to legend, derives from the gifts offered by the Neapolitans to the nymph Parthenope who cheered them with her song. The gifts symbolized what the area had to offer: flour, sugar, orange blossom, wheat, spices, ricotta and eggs. Parthenope, happy to receive these gifts, offered them up to the gods, who mixed them together and created this famous cake.

Abruzzo and Molise both have their own notable desserts, in particular the famous parozzo. Rome has the deliciously light fried choux pastry buns, traditionally prepared on Father's Day, which in Italy falls on 19 March, St Joseph's Day.

TRADIZIONALE
LIQUORE DI LIMONI
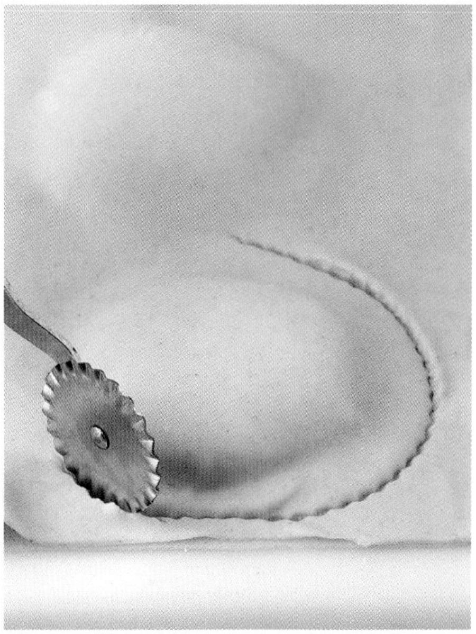

CHRISTMAS CHICKPEA PASTRIES
CAUCIUNE DI NATALE

This Christmas Eve speciality from Molise is from an ancient recipe for little fried pastries with a sweet chocolate and citrus filling, the origin of which is lost in historical rituals. There are two Molisan customs connected with making cauciuni. Firstly, the chickpeas are soaked out of doors overnight, preferably on a frosty night. Secondly, when testing that the oil for frying the pastries is hot enough, it is traditional to make a wish for the coming year while you watch the first small piece of pastry sizzle in the pan.

MAKES ABOUT 30

500g/1¼lb plain (all-purpose) flour, sifted
90ml/6 tbsp olive oil
1.5ml/¼ tsp salt
10ml/2 tsp vanilla extract
60ml/4 tbsp dry white wine
sunflower oil, for deep-frying
45ml/3 tbsp icing (confectioners') sugar
7.5ml/1½ tsp ground cinnamon

FOR THE FILLING

500g/1¼lb dried chickpeas, soaked overnight and drained
45ml/3 tbsp unsweetened cocoa powder
45ml/3 tbsp caster (superfine) sugar
200g/7oz/generous 1 cup chopped candied citrus peel
45ml/3 tbsp clear honey
30ml/2 tbsp sweet liqueur of your choice, Amaretto or Maraschino

1 To make the filling, rinse the soaked chickpeas, then boil them rapidly for 5 minutes in some fresh water. Drain them and rinse once again, then cover with fresh water and simmer slowly for about 3 hours, or until completely tender and almost pulpy.

2 Drain the chickpeas and push them through a food mill or a sieve (strainer) to create a purée.

3 In a large mixing bowl, mix the chickpea purée with the cocoa powder, caster sugar, citrus peel, honey and liqueur, using a wooden spoon, to make a smooth filling. Set the filling aside while you make the pastry, to allow the flavours to develop.

4 To make the pastry, pile all the flour on to the work surface and make a hole in the centre with your fist. Pour the oil into the centre with the salt, vanilla extract and half the wine.

5 Knead the ingredients into the flour, adding the remaining wine, a little at a time, until you have a very smooth, shiny and elastic dough. You may not need all of the wine.

6 Roll the dough out very thinly and cut it into 7.5cm/3in circles using a pastry (cookie) cutter.

7 Put a spoonful of filling on one half of each circle, fold the circles in half and seal them closed using the prongs of a fork.

8 Heat the sunflower oil in a large pan or deep-fryer until a small piece of the pastry, dropped into the oil, sizzles and browns almost immediately.

9 Fry the cauciuni in batches of four or five at a time. As soon as they are puffy and golden brown, remove them from the hot oil using a slotted spoon. Drain them carefully on kitchen paper and keep them warm while you cook the rest.

10 Dust generously with icing sugar and cinnamon, and serve piping hot.

PER PASTRY Energy 131kcal/544kJ; Protein 3.4g; Carbohydrate 5.6g, of which sugars 1.2g; Fat 10.7g, of which saturates 5.5g; Cholesterol 48mg; Calcium 7mg; Fibre 0.4g; Sodium 261mg.

SARDINIAN HONEY FRITTERS
SEBADAS

These sticky and sweet ravioli fritters are called sebadas and are a classic dessert from the unique and beautiful island of Sardinia. They are traditionally filled with local creamy sheep's milk cheese (but any cream cheese can be used instead) and drizzled with fragrant orange blossom honey. They are one of the typical sweet recipes of the mountainous, sparsely populated area of Barbagia, which is located just south of the central part of the island.

SERVES 8

500g/1¼lb plain (all-purpose) flour, plus extra for dusting
45ml/3 tbsp lard or white cooking fat
a pinch of salt
sunflower oil, for deep-frying
60ml/4 tbsp clear honey
grated rind of 1 lemon

FOR THE FILLING

500g/1¼lb/5 cups cream cheese
250ml/8fl oz/1 cup boiling water
a pinch of salt
grated rind of 1 lemon
30ml/2 tbsp fine semolina

1 To make the filling, put the cream cheese in a small pan and mix with the boiling water, salt and lemon rind. Simmer gently, stirring with a whisk, until the mixture is smooth and creamy.

2 Add the semolina and whisk until it has become a thick paste. Remove from the heat and leave to cool.

3 Dip your hands in cold water and shape the mixture into little flat pancakes about 6cm/2½in in diameter and about 1cm/½in thick.

4 Line a baking tray with baking parchment. Lay the pancakes out in one layer on the tray, well spaced out. Use a clean dish cloth to dab any excess moisture off them. You can lay a sheet of baking parchment over the pancakes and arrange another layer of pancakes on top, if you are short of space. These are the fillings.

5 To make the pastry, pile all the flour on to the work surface and make a hole in the centre. Add the lard or white cooking fat and salt. Knead together, adding enough tepid water to make a smooth, elastic dough.

6 Put the dough in a plastic bag and rest it in the refrigerator for about 15 minutes.

7 Divide the dough in half. On a floured surface, roll out each piece very thinly to make two even sheets. Lay the sebadas on one sheet of dough, evenly spaced and side-by-side in rows.

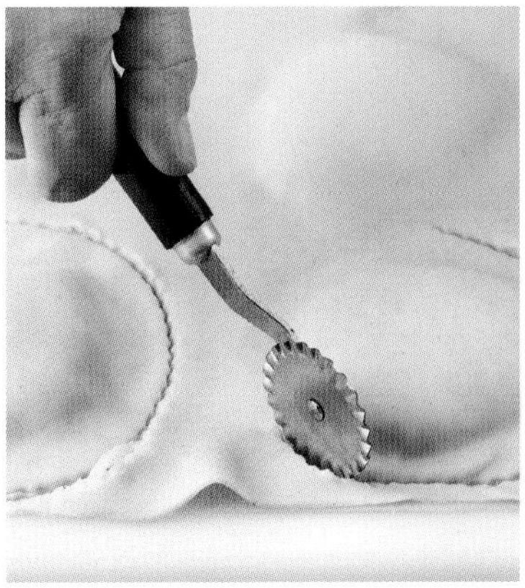

8 Lay the other sheet of dough on top and gently roll the rolling pin around the edges to seal. Using a pastry wheel or a 7.5cm/3in pastry (cookie) cutter, cut around each sebadas pancake, leaving a narrow edge of pastry.

9 Heat the sunflower oil in a large pan or deep-fryer until a small cube of bread, dropped in the oil, sizzles instantly. Fry the pastries in batches until golden.

10 Remove the pastries using a slotted spoon, and drain on kitchen paper. Serve hot, drizzled with honey and sprinkled with lemon rind.

PER PORTION Energy 672kcal/2796kJ; Protein 8.3g; Carbohydrate 57.2g, of which sugars 6.6g; Fat 47.2g, of which saturates 22.3g; Cholesterol 65mg; Calcium 150mg; Fibre 2g; Sodium 191mg.

SARDINIAN ICED COOKIES
PAPASSINAS

These deliciously nutty, fruity little biscuits are another speciality of picturesque Sardinia and go perfectly with a glass or two of local Moscato wine. They contain a tasty mix of walnuts, almonds, pine nuts, raisins and candied peel, and are traditionally coated with pure white icing, topped with pretty coloured sugar sprinkles. Throughout Sardinia you will find these local sweet treats on sale in all good bakeries and cake shops.

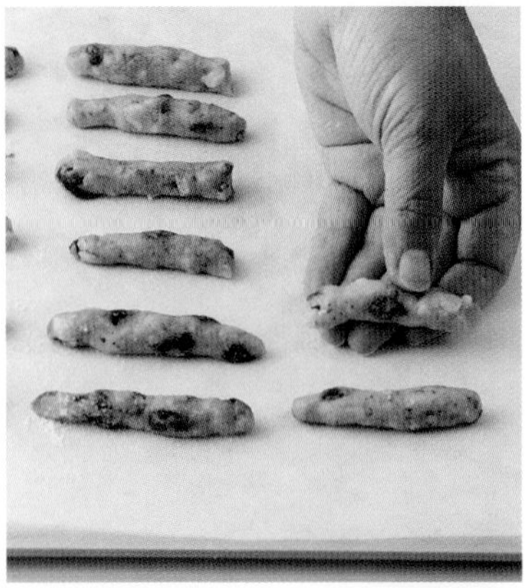

1 First, begin to make the icing. Place the caster sugar in a heatproof bowl with 45ml/3 tbsp cold water, and set over a pan of simmering water. Stir continuously until the sugar has dissolved completely, then remove the bowl from the simmering water and set aside to cool a little.

2 Preheat the oven to 180°C/350°F/Gas 4, and line a baking sheet with baking parchment.

3 Sift the flour and baking powder into a large bowl and stir in the eggs and the sugar with a wooden spoon until smooth.

4 Gradually mix in the lard or white cooking fat, nuts, raisins or sultanas, pine nuts and candied orange peel. Work this dough with your hands until it is compact and even.

5 Shape the dough into sticks 1cm/½in wide and 6cm/2½in long and arrange them on the prepared baking sheet.

6 Bake the pastries for 10 minutes, or until they are lightly golden. Transfer them to a cooling rack while you finish the icing.

7 Put the egg whites into a clean, grease-free bowl and whisk until they form stiff peaks. Gently fold them into the cooled sugar syrup until you have created a shiny, glassy icing.

8 When the baked biscuits are cooled, brush them with the icing, then sprinkle them with the coloured sugar sprinkles. Allow the icing to set, then serve.

SERVES 10 TO 12

- 500g/1¼lb/4¼ cups plain (all-purpose) flour
- 5ml/1 tsp baking powder
- 4 eggs, beaten
- 150g/5oz caster (superfine) sugar
- 200g/7oz/generous 1 cup lard or white cooking fat, softened
- 250g/9oz/2¼ cups chopped walnuts
- 250g/9oz/2¼ cups blanched chopped almonds
- 250g/9oz/scant 2 cups raisins or sultanas (golden raisins), soaked for 20 minutes in warm water and drained
- 200g/7oz/scant 2 cups pine nuts
- 115g/4oz/⅔ cup finely chopped candied orange peel

FOR THE ICING

- 300g/11oz/generous 1½ cups caster (superfine) sugar
- 2 egg whites
- 15ml/1 tbsp coloured sugar sprinkles

PER PORTION Energy 881kcal/3676kJ; Protein 17g; Carbohydrate 81g, of which sugars 48.9g; Fat 56.4, of which saturates 10.3g; Cholesterol 79mg; Calcium 191mg; Fibre 4.7g; Sodium 72mg.

ABRUZZESE RING COOKIES
CIAMBELLINE ABRUZZESI

Designed specifically to be dunked, these unusual ring-shaped biscuits are hard in texture so that they won't disintegrate when dipped into wine at the end of a meal. They are especially delicious dunked into frothy, milky coffee for an Italian breakfast.

1 In a large mixing bowl, mix the sugar, wine and oil together using a whisk. Gradually beat in the flour until you have a pliable, kneadable dough. You may not need all of the flour so just add it a little at a time.

2 Transfer the ball of dough to a bowl, cover with a cloth, and leave to rest in the refrigerator for at least 30 minutes.

3 Preheat the oven to 160°C/325°F/ Gas 3 and grease a baking sheet with the lard or fat.

4 Roll the dough into 10cm/4in long sausage shapes on a floured surface. Bend them round to form rings. Arrange on the baking sheet.

5 Bake for 20 minutes, then cool on a wire rack. Serve with coffee, if you like.

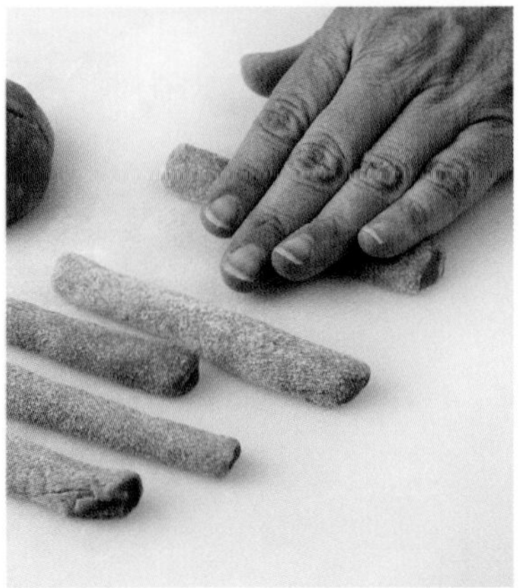

SERVES 6 TO 8

115g/4oz/generous $1/2$ cup caster (superfine) sugar
100ml/3$1/2$fl oz/scant $1/2$ cup red wine
100ml/3$1/2$fl oz/scant $1/2$ cup olive oil
about 250g/9oz/2$1/4$ cups plain (all-purpose) flour
15ml/1 tbsp lard or white cooking fat

PER PORTION Energy 275kcal/1155kJ; Protein 3g; Carbohydrate 39.3g, of which sugars 15.5g; Fat 11.9g, of which saturates 2.2g; Cholesterol 1.7mg; Calcium 52mg; Fibre 0.9g; Sodium 3.1mg.

MAKES ABOUT 24 BUNS

130g/4½oz/generous ½ cup unsalted butter
250ml/8fl oz/1 cup cold water
150g/5oz/1¼ cups plain (all-purpose) flour
4 eggs, beaten
sunflower oil, for deep-frying
caster (superfine) sugar, icing (confectioners') sugar, or a mixture of cornflour (cornstarch) and cinnamon, for dusting

ST JOSEPH'S DAY CHOUX BUNS
BIGNE' DI SAN GIUSEPPE

The story goes that St Joseph, husband to the Virgin Mary and, in Italy, the patron saint of fathers, was a carpenter and would always have enough leftover wood to build a fire to cook on. According to the story, many carpenters of that time had a sideline in selling fried street food as a way of supplementing their income from carpentry, and would offer simple food to passers-by, such as the famous bigne'. These buns are traditionally eaten on St Joseph's Day, which is also Father's Day in Italy.

1 Put the butter in a pan with the water. Heat until the butter has melted and then bring to the boil. Add the flour all at once and stir constantly with a wooden spoon. Cook for 2 minutes, or until the mixture pulls away from the sides of the pan, forming a ball.

2 Remove from the heat and allow to cool. Wrap the dough in clear film (plastic wrap) and chill in the refrigerator for 30 minutes.

3 Transfer the dough to a bowl. Using a wooden spoon or the paddle attachment of a food processor or mixer, mix the dough for 1–2 minutes.

4 Gradually add the beaten eggs, mixing the dough until smooth each time. Scrape down the sides of the bowl. The dough should be soft and glossy, but able to hold its shape.

5 Heat the sunflower oil in a large pan or deep-fryer until a cube of bread, dropped into the oil, sizzles instantly. Using two teaspoons, scoop balls of the mixture into the hot oil. Leave until they are puffy and golden. Remove with a slotted spoon and drain on kitchen paper.

6 Lightly toss the cooked buns in caster sugar, icing sugar, or a mixture of cornflour and cinnamon, and serve warm.

VARIATION

Snip the base of the buns open with scissors and fill (using a clean piping bag) with confectioner's custard, zabaglione, whipped cream or melted chocolate.

PER BUN Energy 106kcal/441kJ; Protein 1.7g; Carbohydrate 4.9g, of which sugars 0.1g; Fat 9.1g, of which saturates 3.6g; Cholesterol 44mg; Calcium 14mg; Fibre 0.2g; Sodium 53mg.

NEAPOLITAN EASTER CAKE
LA PASTIERA

This time-honoured cake originates in the city of Naples and the surrounding region of Campania, and dates back many centuries to ancient Rome. It was traditionally made to symbolize fertility and was always baked to celebrate the beginning of spring. Today it is an essential part of the Easter feast for all Neapolitans. It is quite an unusual recipe as it is made with cooked wheat grain. You should be able to find this in specialist delicatessens, but if not you can substitute it (see Cook's Tip).

SERVES 8 TO 12

400g/14oz cooked wheat grain (see Cook's Tip)
100ml/3½fl oz/scant ½ cup milk
30g/1¼oz unsalted butter, plus extra for greasing
grated rind of 1 lemon
675g/1½lb/3 cups ricotta cheese
600g/1lb 5oz/3 cups caster (superfine) sugar
5 eggs, plus 3 egg yolks
10ml/2 tsp vanilla extract
15nl/1 tbsp orange flower water
a pinch of ground cinnamon
50g/2oz glacé (candied) citron, chopped
50g/2oz candied orange peel, chopped
50g/2oz mixed glacé (candied) fruit, chopped
1kg/2¼lb shortcrust pastry
plain (all-purpose) flour, for dusting
icing (confectioners') sugar, for dusting

1 Preheat the oven to 180°C/350°F/Gas 4 and generously grease a 30cm/12in diameter flan tin (pan) with butter.

2 Put the wheat grain into a pan and add the milk, butter and grated lemon rind. Simmer slowly over a low heat for about 10 minutes, or until creamy.

3 In a mixing bowl, whisk together the ricotta cheese, sugar, the 5 eggs and 2 of the egg yolks, the vanilla, orange flower water and cinnamon.

4 Work this mixture together until smooth, and then mix in the glacé fruit and candied peel, and the creamy grain.

5 Roll out the pastry on a floured surface to about 5mm/¼in thick and use to line the flan tin. Cut all the excess pastry into 1cm/½in wide, 30cm/12in long strips to make the lattice topping of your pastiera. Set aside.

6 Beat the remaining egg yolk. Pour the ricotta and grain mixture into the tart case and arrange the strips of pastry over the top in a lattice pattern.

7 Brush the pastry with the beaten egg yolk. Bake for 1½ hours, or until golden brown. Remove from the oven and leave to cool.

8 Sprinkle the pastiera lightly with icing sugar just before serving. Once baked, the pastiera can be kept in the refrigerator for 3 days, during which time it will improve daily.

COOK'S TIP

You will find canned wheat grain in Italian delicatessens. Alternatively, soak raw wheat grain in cold water for 2 days, changing the water twice a day, then boil gently for up to an hour, until softened. Wheat grain is sold in health food shops; however, if it is impossible to find, substitute with either pearl barley (soaked overnight in cold water then drained and boiled in fresh water for 30 minutes) or boiled pudding rice (cooked for 20 minutes in water).

PER PORTION Energy 809kcal/3396kJ; Protein 14.7g; Carbohydrate 110g, of which sugars 62.6g; Fat 37.6g, of which saturates 16g; Cholesterol 190mg; Calcium 144mg; Fibre 2.2g; Sodium 435mg.

CHOCOLATE-COVERED ALMOND CAKE
PARROZZO ABRUZZESE

The name of this superb cake derives from 'pan rozzo', a simple bread made by Abruzzese shepherds from ground corn, water and a little olive oil. In 1920, a baker called Luigi D'Amico, from the coastal town of Pescara, took this rather characterless example of cucina povera (or 'the poor kitchen'), and elevated it by adding plenty of ground sweet almonds from Abruzzo's abundant almond groves and embellishing it with a coating of rich chocolate. Its popularity spread beyond Pescara, and Parrozzo is now one of the iconic sweets of the region. The controversial poet and writer Gabriel D'Annunzio, a native of Pescara, was so inspired by its unique flavours that he composed a poem about it, 'Song of the Parrozzo'.

1 Preheat the oven to 180°C/350°F/Gas 4 and grease a 23cm/9in cake tin (pan). Put the almonds and 40g/1½oz sugar in a mortar and pound with a pestle into a fine powder. Alternatively, you can use a food processor.

2 Melt the butter in a heatproof bowl set over a pan of simmering water, then leave it to cool without letting it harden.

3 Put the egg yolks in a large bowl and whisk, gradually adding the remaining sugar, until light and fluffy. Gradually add the almond mixture alternately with the flour, cornflour and melted butter, stirring constantly.

4 Put the egg whites into a clean, grease-free bowl and whisk until they form stiff peaks. Fold them gently into the mixture.

5 Pour the cake mixture into the prepared tin and bake for 40 minutes, or until a knife inserted into the centre comes out clean. Allow to cool in the tin for 15 minutes, and then turn out on to a wire rack to cool completely.

6 Melt the chocolate in a heatproof bowl set over a pan of simmering water, then use it to cover the top of the cake, spreading it evenly with a metal spatula. Allow the chocolate to harden, then serve.

SERVES 6 TO 8

75g/3oz/½ cup blanched almonds
130g/4½oz/scant ¾ cup caster (superfine) sugar
75g/3oz/6 tbsp unsalted butter, plus extra for greasing
5 eggs, separated
50g/2oz/½ cup plain (all-purpose) flour
50g/2oz/½ cup cornflour (cornstarch)
150g/5oz cooking chocolate

PER PORTION 316kcal/1318kJ; Protein 7.4g; Carbohydrate 23.9g, of which sugars 12.2g; Fat 21.9g, of which saturates 9.7g; Cholesterol 142mg; Calcium 59mg; Fibre 0.9g; Sodium 121mg.

SERVES 8

250g/9oz/generous 1 cup unsalted butter, plus extra for greasing
6 eggs, separated
250g/9oz/$1\frac{1}{4}$ cups caster (superfine) sugar
60ml/4 tbsp Limoncello
400g/14oz/$2\frac{1}{3}$ cups blanched almonds, finely chopped
300g/11oz plain (semisweet) chocolate, grated
icing (confectioners') sugar, for dusting

PER PORTION Energy 931kcal/3875kJ; Protein 17.3g; Carbohydrate 62.9g, of which sugars 59.5g; Fat 68.6g, of which saturates 26.7g; Cholesterol 218mg; Calcium 177mg; Fibre 3.7g; Sodium 301mg.

CAPRESE CAKE
TORTA CAPRESE

This delicious chocolate and almond cake is sticky and moreish, but light at the same time. You can alter the flavour by using a different liqueur, such as Maraschino, though Limoncello is the most traditional liqueur to use.

1 Preheat the oven to 180°C/350°F/Gas 4. Grease a 20cm/8in cake tin (pan), then line with baking parchment. Melt the butter in a heatproof bowl set over a pan of simmering water. Remove from the heat and leave to cool.

2 Whisk the egg yolks and sugar together with the Limoncello until light and fluffy. Fold in the melted butter, the chopped almonds and chocolate.

3 Put the egg whites into a clean, grease-free bowl and whisk until they form stiff peaks. Fold into the cake mixture.

4 Transfer to the prepared tin and bake for 50 minutes, or until a knife inserted into the centre of the cake comes out clean.

5 Leave to cool on a wire rack, and then dust generously with icing sugar to serve.

CIVITAVECCHIA CAKE

PIZZA DOLCE DI CIVITAVECCHIA

This rich yeast cake is from Civitavecchia, a coastal town in the province of Rome. It is flavoured with plenty of chocolate and a good splash of rum. Start preparations the day before, as at the first stage, the dough will need to rise throughout the night. The cake will have three rising stages in total, so it is quite a time-consuming recipe to make. The finished cake, drizzled with luxurious chocolate, is a real treat, and well worth the time spent making it.

SERVES 8

- 50g/2oz fresh yeast
- 45ml/3 tbsp warm water
- 115g/4oz/1 cup, plus 300g/11oz/ $2\frac{3}{4}$ cups, plain (all-purpose) flour, plus extra for dusting
- 375g/13oz best-quality cooking chocolate
- 7 egg yolks
- 150g/5oz/$\frac{3}{4}$ cup caster (superfine) sugar
- 50g/2oz/$\frac{1}{4}$ cup ricotta cheese
- 45ml/3 tbsp dark rum
- 115g/4oz/$\frac{2}{3}$ cup lard or white cooking fat, cubed
- 45ml/3 tbsp sunflower oil, for greasing
- 45ml/3 tbsp icing (confectioners') sugar, sifted

1 Cream the yeast in the warm water and mix into the 115g/4oz/1 cup plain flour to make a small ball of dough. Put in a bowl and cover with a damp cloth. Leave in a warm place to rise overnight.

2 The next day, melt 250g/9oz chocolate in a heatproof bowl set over a pan of gently simmering water. Remove the bowl from the heat and set aside, but do not allow it to harden.

3 In a bowl, beat 6 of the egg yolks with the sugar, using a whisk, until pale and light. Beat in the ricotta cheese and the rum, then carefully stir in the melted chocolate using a wooden spoon.

4 Add this mixture to the bowl containing the risen ball of dough and knead together lightly to incorporate the mixture into the dough.

5 Add the remaining flour and the lard or white fat, and knead until the dough comes together.

6 Put the dough on a work surface and knead everything together very thoroughly. Transfer the dough to a bowl, cover with a damp cloth and leave to rise for 1 hour or until doubled in volume.

7 Grease a 28cm/11in cake tin (pan) with the sunflower oil. Put the dough on a floured work surface. Knock back (punch down) the dough, then transfer it into the prepared cake tin.

8 Place the tin in a warm place to rise for 1 hour or until the dough has risen above the top of the tin.

9 Preheat the oven to 160°C/325°F/Gas 3. Beat the remaining egg yolk and use it to brush the top of the risen dough. Dust with icing sugar and bake for 45 minutes, or until golden and firm.

10 Cool the cake in the tin, then turn out on to a platter. Melt the remaining chocolate in a heatproof bowl set over a pan of gently simmering water. Drizzle over the cake and allow to harden before serving.

PER PORTION Energy 761kcal/3187kJ; Protein 10.3g; Carbohydrate 96.4g, of which sugars 54.3g; Fat 38.4g, of which saturates 16.3g; Cholesterol 197mg; Calcium 124mg; Fibre 1.6g; Sodium 16mg.

INDEX

PUBLISHER'S ACKNOWLEDGEMENTS
The publisher would like to thank the following for permission to reproduce their images: 7tl Sandro Vannini/Corbis; 7tr ML Sinibaldi/Corbis; 7b Jon Arnold Images Ltd/Alamy; 9t Philippe Giraud/Sygma/Corbis; 9bl Bildarchiv Monheim GmbH/Alamy; 9br Robert Harding Picture Library Ltd/Alamy; 10bl Robin Chapman/Alamy; 10br foodfolio/Alamy; 11tl adam eastland/Alamy; 11tr Bettman/Corbis; 12tl, 13bl and 13br CuboImages srl/Alamy; 12tr Hulton-Deutsch Collection/Corbis; 15tl theodore liasi/Alamy; 15tr vittorio sciosia/Alamy; 8, 14, 34, 40, 54, 58, 60, 71, 72, 88, 106, 112, 115, 116, 124 iStockphoto.